D1191879

BASIC WITH STYLE

PROGRAMMING
PROVERBS

PAUL NAGIN
AND
HENRY F. LEDGARD

HAYDEN

Principles of *Good Programming*
with Numerous Examples to
Improve Programming *Style* and *Proficiency*

BASIC WITH STYLE

PROGRAMMING PROVERBS

Hayden Computer Programming Series

COMPREHENSIVE STANDARD FORTRAN PROGRAMMING
James N. Haag

BASICS OF DIGITAL COMPUTER PROGRAMMING (Second Ed.)
John S. Murphy

BASIC BASIC: An Introduction to Computer Programming in BASIC Language (Second Ed.)
James S. Coan

ADVANCED BASIC: Applications and Problems
James S. Coan

DISCOVERING BASIC: A Problem Solving Approach
Robert E. Smith

ASSEMBLY LANGUAGE BASICS: An Annotated Program Book
Irving A. Dodes

PROGRAMMING PROVERBS
Henry F. Ledgard

PROGRAMMING PROVERBS FOR FORTRAN PROGRAMMERS
Henry F. Ledgard

FORTRAN WITH STYLE: Programming Proverbs
Henry F. Ledgard and Louis J. Chmura

COBOL WITH STYLE: Programming Proverbs
Louis J. Chmura and Henry F. Ledgard

BASIC WITH STYLE: Programming Proverbs
Paul Nagin and Henry F. Ledgard

SNOBOL: An Introduction to Programming
Peter R. Newsted

FORTRAN FUNDAMENTALS: A Short Course
Jack Steingraber

THE BASIC WORKBOOK: Creative Techniques for Beginning Programmers
Kenneth E. Schoman, Jr.

BASIC FROM THE GROUND UP
David E. Simon

APL: AN INTRODUCTION
Howard A. Peelle

88526

BASIC WITH STYLE

PROVERBS

PAUL A. NAGIN
University of Massachusetts

HENRY F. LEDGARD
University of Massachusetts

005.13
B292n

discarded

HAYDEN BOOK COMPANY, INC.
Rochelle Park, New Jersey

MERNER-PFEIFFER LIBRARY
TENNESSEE WESLEYAN COLLEGE
ATHENS, TN 37303

Library of Congress Cataloging in Publication Data

Nagin, Paul A
    BASIC with style.

    (Hayden computer programming series)
    Bibliography: p.
    Includes index.
    1. Basic (Computer program language) I. Ledgard,
Henry F., 1943-   joint author. II. Title.
QA76.73.B3N33   001.6'424   78-12663
ISBN 0-8104-5115-8

Copyright © 1978 by HAYDEN BOOK COMPANY, INC. All rights reserved.
No part of this book may be reprinted, or reproduced, or utilized in any
form or by any electronic, mechanical, or other means, now known or
hereafter invented, including photocopying and recording, or in any information storage and retrieval system, without permission in writing from
the Publisher.

Printed in the United States of America

    2   3   4   5   6   7   8   9   PRINTING

    79 80 81 82 83 84 85 86   YEAR

FEB 1 '80

FOREWORD

By necessity, computer science, computer education, and computer practice are all embryonic human activities, for they have existed for only a single generation. From the beginning, programming has been a frustrating black art, with individual abilities ranging from the excellent to the ridiculous and often exhibiting very little in the way of systematic mental procedure. In a sense, the teaching of programming through mistakes and debugging can hardly be regarded as legitimate university level course work. At the university level we teach such topics as the notion of an algorithm, concepts in programming languages, compiler design, operating systems, information storage and retrieval, artificial intelligence, and numerical computation; but in order to implement ideas in any of these functional activities, we need to write programs in a specific language.

Students and professionals alike tend to be overly optimistic about their ability to write programs or to make programs work according to preestablished design goals. However, we are beginning to see a breakthrough in programming as a mental process. This breakthrough is based more on considerations of style than on detail. It involves taking style seriously, not only in how programs look when they are completed, but in the very mental processes that create them. In programming, it is not enough to be inventive and ingenious. One also needs to be disciplined and controlled in order not to become entangled in one's own complexities.

In any new area of human activity, it is difficult to foresee latent human capabilities. We have many examples of such capabilities: touch typing, speed writing, and 70-year-old grandmothers who drive down our highways at 70 miles an hour. Back in 1900 it was possible to foresee cars going 70 miles an hour, but the drivers were imagined as daredevils rather than as grandmothers. The moral is that in any new human activity one generation hardly scratches the surface of its capabilities. So it will be in programming as well.

The next generation of programmers will be much more competent than the first one. They will have to be. Just as it was easier to get into college in the "good old days," it was also easier to get by as a programmer in the "good old days." For this new generation, a programmer will need to be capable of a level of precision and productivity never dreamed of before.

This new generation of programmers will need to acquire discipline and control, mainly by learning to write programs correctly from the start. The debugging process will take the new form of verifying that no errors are present, rather than the old form of finding and fixing errors over and over (otherwise known as "acquiring confidence by exhaustion"). Programming is a serious logical business that requires concentration and precision. In this discipline, concentration is highly related to confidence.

In simple illustration, consider a child who knows how to play a perfect game of tic-tac-toe but does not know that he knows. If you ask him to play for something important, like a candy bar, he will say to himself, "I hope I can win." And sometimes he will win, and sometimes not. The only reason he does not always win is that he drops his concentration. He does not realize this fact because he regards winning as a chance event. Consider how different the situation is when the child *knows* that he knows how to play a perfect game of tic-tac-toe. Now he does not say, "I hope I can win." He says instead, "I know I can win; it's up to me!" And he recognizes the necessity for concentration in order to insure that he wins.

In programming, as in tic-tac-toe, it is characteristic that concentration goes hand in hand with justified confidence in one's own ability. It is not enough simply to know how to write programs correctly. The programmer must *know that he knows* how to write programs correctly, and then supply the concentration to match.

This book of proverbs is well suited to getting members of the next generation off to the right start. The elements of style discussed here can help provide the mental discipline to master programming complexity. In essence, the book can help a programmer make a large first step on the road to a new generation of programming.

HARLAN D. MILLS

Federal Systems Division, IBM
Gaithersburg, Maryland

PREFACE

This text was motivated by a small book called *Elements of Style*, written by William Strunk, Jr., and revised by E. B. White. Originally conceived in 1918, Strunk's book stressed the need for rigor, conciseness, and clarity in the writing of English prose. In like manner, this text is intended for BASIC programmers who want to write carefully constructed, readable programs.

Many programmers have told us of programming experiences in which a simple set of guidelines could have averted disaster. Although a burned hand may teach a good lesson, we believe that the introduction of well-advised guidelines is an easier and less painful way to achieve good programming. To be sure, rules of style restrict the programmer. However, our hope is to enable the programmer to focus creativity on the deeper issues in programming rather than on problems that obscure the issues.

Several characteristics other than academic ones have been deliberately sought in this book. First, there has been an attempt to be lighthearted. The intention is to encourage a zest for learning that we all need in order to do our more rewarding work. Second, there has been an attempt to be specific. Progress is made when we speak plainly and give examples of what we say.

The programming examples are given in BASIC, but the points of the examples should be clear even without a detailed knowledge of the BASIC language. In particular, the programs given here generally conform to the recently proposed American National Standard version of the BASIC language [Ref. Z1]*. Those readers familiar only with a particular implementation of BASIC will notice some differences.

This book is designed as a guide to better programming, not as an introduction to the details of BASIC or a similar higher level language. It should be of value to all programmers who have some familiarity with BASIC. As such, it may be used as a supplementary text in courses where BASIC programming is a major concern, or as an informal guide to experienced programmers who have an interest in improving software quality. However, we strongly believe that the ideas presented should go hand in hand with learning the BASIC language itself.

---

*See the Bibliography at the conclusion of the text for all references.

The reader who dismisses the overall objective of this book with the comment, "I've got to learn all about BASIC first," may be surprised to find that the study of good programming practices in conjunction with the basics of the language may reap quick and longstanding rewards.

BASIC with Style is organized in five major parts. Chapter 1 is an opening statement. Chapter 2 is a collection of simple rules, called *proverbs*. The proverbs summarize in terse form the major ideas of this book. Each proverb is explained and applied. There are a few references to later chapters where various ideas are more fully explored.

Chapter 3 is an introduction to a strict top-down approach for programming problems in any programming language. The approach is oriented toward the easy writing of complete, correct, readable programs. It should be read carefully, because some of its details are critical and not necessarily intuitive. The approach hinges on developing the overall logical structure of the program first.

Chapter 4 gives a set of strict program standards for writing programs. These rules have been strictly followed in this book, and we believe that their adoption is one of the most important factors in achieving quality programs. Chapter 5 elaborates on several important and sometimes controversial ideas discussed in the chapter on programming proverbs.

This effort has been aided by many individuals. Louis Chmura, Andrew Singer, Michael Marcotty, and Jon Hueras deeply influenced our thinking. Louis Chmura, co-author of *COBOL with Style,* provided the nucleus of many ideas for this book as well and launched the story of Dorothy and Irene. Andrew Singer was the source of a stimulating critique of the whole area of programming and is the best programmer and program designer we have ever met. Jon Hueras provided an example of superb programming in a practical setting. Michael Marcotty set an example of eloquent programming style and often contributed the right word at the right time.

Edwina Carter and Linda Strzegowski provided services without which this book would be but a collection of handwritten pages. William Fastie, Joseph Davison, and Leslie Chaikin were the sources of many ideas taken from the predecessors of this book. Members of the Computer and Information Science Department at the University of Massachusetts provided a solid intellectual environment for this work. We are grateful to all.

BASIC with Style is surely our own personal statement about programming. Other views have been given by Kernighan and Plauger [Ref. K1], Van Tassel [Ref. V1], and Kreitzberg and Schneiderman [Ref. K2]. Nevertheless, we firmly believe that the study of guidelines for good programming can be of great value to all programmers and that there are principles that transcend the techniques of any individual practitioner.

PAUL A. NAGIN
HENRY F. LEDGARD

CONTENTS

CHAPTER ONE
THE WAY AHEAD

Things is 'round to help learn BASIC programmers, especially them who don't want to pick up no more bad habits, to program good, easy, the first time right, and so somebody else can figger out what they done and why.

For those readers who appreciate diamonds in the rough, the paragraph above represents all that follows.

An indication of the current state of the art of computer programming is that the proud exclamation, "It worked the first time!," is rarely heard. Writing programs that work correctly the first time is possible, but unusual. Since programmers undoubtedly try to write programs that work the first time, one wonders why they don't succeed more often. The reasons are simple. First, programming is difficult. Second, there are very few principles for developing and writing good programs. Since few principles exist, each programmer must develop individual ones, often haphazardly.

The reader may well ask, "Why should programs work right the first time?" The reason is not at all obvious. Less compiler time? Less debugging time? Fewer hours at the terminal? Not really. Imagine for the moment that you had to buy one of two computer programs, each 10,000 lines long. Let us not quibble about the cost but assume that the costs are for all purposes equal, about a hundred thousand dollars. Let's even suppose that each program has been thoroughly tested and certified to be absolutely correct. Now imagine that the only other thing you know about the programs is that the first required hundreds of modifications but that the second worked right the first time! Which program would you buy? And *why?*

In reality, the state of the art is considerably worse than the fact that most programs do not work right the first time. Too many programs work only most of the time. Indeed, a few never work at all. What's more, of those that do work correctly, many are laborious to maintain.

1

Over past years there has been an increasing concern within the computing community about the quality of software. As a result, a new methodology is emerging, a harbinger of further changes to come. Notable are the works of Weinberg, Mills, Dijkstra, Wirth, Hoare, Wulf, Horning, Parnas, Cave, Strachey, Kosaraju, Knuth, and Marcotty. Many of the developing ideas are already very useful. The time has come for programmers to write programs that work correctly the first time. Programs should do the whole job, even if the original problem has been poorly conceived. Programs should be easy to read, understand, and maintain.

For those accustomed to poor program performance, weeks of testing, or long hours deciphering someone else's code, the above statements might seem unrealistic. Nevertheless, there are well-founded principles that can be utilized to achieve these goals. Some of the principles we shall present are obvious, even to novice programmers. Others even experienced programmers might debate. However, before any principle is rejected, it must be remembered that a program is not only a set of descriptions and instructions for a computer, but a *set of descriptions and instructions that must be understood by human beings, especially the one who reads it the most—you, the programmer.*

It is well known that the cost of program development and maintenance today is high and growing. In fact, we have heard it said that the cost of program maintenance on some poorly constructed systems is a hundred times greater than the cost of initial development and testing. To attack these costs, methodology and clarity must be early programming concerns.

In view of today's increasing development and maintenance costs and the decreasing costs of computer hardware it is shortsighted to be overconcerned with various "micro-efficiency" [Ref. A1] techniques that save bytes and milliseconds. The considerations of an "efficient" computer program can no longer ignore overall program costs.

The use of flowcharting as a program development and documentation technique also has been misunderstood and overestimated. A case against program flowcharts is given in Chapter 5. While judicious use of certain types of flowcharts can be a valuable part of the programmer's repertoire, there are numerous other programming techniques that have little need for flowcharts. The reader will observe a scarcity of program flowcharts in this book.

The development of effective algorithms and data structures is an activity that is closely related to general programming techniques. While general programming techniques can offer strong guidelines for the development of a good solution, they will not necessarily help the programmer determine the best data organization scheme, the best numerical algorithm, or the clearest output of results. So advised, we shall proceed to make our case.

CHAPTER TWO
PROGRAMMING PROVERBS

"Experience keeps a dear school, but fools will learn in no other."
Maxim prefixed to *Poor Richard's Almanack,* 1757

Over two centuries ago Ben Franklin published his now familiar *Poor Richard's Almanack.* In it he collected a number of maxims meant as a simple guide to everyday living. Similarly, this chapter is intended as a simple guide to everyday BASIC programming. As such, it contains a collection of terse statements that serve as a set of practical rules for the BASIC programmer. These programming proverbs motivate the entire book.

Before going on, a prefatory proverb seems appropriate:

Do Not Break the Rules Before Learning Them

As with most maxims or proverbs, the rules are not absolute, but neither are they arbitrary. Behind each one lies a generous nip of thought and experience. We hope the programmer will seriously consider them. At first glance some of them may seem either trivial or too time-consuming to follow. However, we believe that experience will prove the point. Just take a look at past errors, and then reconsider the proverbs.

The programming proverbs, like all old saws, overlook much important detail in favor of easily remembered phrases. Indeed there are some cases where programs should not conform to standard rules; that is, there are exceptions to every proverb. Nevertheless, we think experience will show that these exceptions are rare and that a programmer should not violate the rules without serious reasons.

A list of all the proverbs is given in Table 2.1. It is hard to weigh their relative importance, but they do at least fall into certain categories. The relative importance of one proverb over another depends quite markedly on the programming problem at hand.

3

Table 2.1   The Programming Proverbs

A Good Start Is Half the Race

1.   Don't Panic!
2.   Define the Problem Completely.
3.   Start the Documentation Early.
4.   Think First. Code Later.
5.   Proceed Top-Down.
6.   Beware of Other Approaches.

Keeping Logical Structure

7.   Code in Logical Units.
8.   Use Functions and Subroutines.
9.   Watch out for GOTOs.
10.   Prettyprint.

Coding the Program

11.   Comment Effectively.
12.   Get the Syntax Correct Now.
13.   Don't Leave the Reader in the Dust.
14.   Produce Good Output.
15.   Hand-Check the Program.
16.   Prepare to Prove the Pudding.

And of Course . . .

17.   Have Someone Else Read the Work.
18.   Read the Manuals Again.
19.   Don't Be Afraid to Start Over!

We close this introduction by noting why we use the word *proverb,* rather than the more accurate word *maxim.* Proverbs and maxims both refer to pithy sayings derived from practical experience. Proverbs are usually well known, whereas maxims are usually not. Admittedly, programming proverbs are not popular sayings. However, the title was chosen with an eye to the future, when hopefully some of these sayings might become true programming proverbs. And, of course, we think that ''Programming Proverbs'' just sounds better!

Proverb 1   DON'T PANIC

This is the first, but often overlooked, programming proverb. When given a new problem to solve, there are many forces that encourage the programmer to abandon thoughtful and effective programming techniques in favor of quicker, high-pressure, unproven ones. Typically, the programmer may be loaded down with other work. Your instructor or manager may be putting on added pressure by setting an unrealistic schedule or by promising a bonus for finishing early. Of course, there is always the natural human tendency to "get on with the job," or in other words, code. Unfortunately, the tendency to try to obtain speedy results is counter to good programming practice.

At the beginning of a programming project, the programmer's good sense must prevail. He or she must develop a thoughtful approach that ensures that the entire programming job is firmly in hand. Not doing so will surely result in a programming environment that is all too common today, where existing code is constantly being reworked, new code reveals oversights, bugs hide all over the finished code, and maintenance takes much longer than expected.

If you find yourself upset or ploughing ahead with a new programming assignment,

1. Stop
2. Calm down
3. Return to methodical programming techniques.

We can't emphasize this enough! One of us, in fact, wanted to go further and retitle this proverb "TAKE THE AFTERNOON OFF," but you know what happens to ideas like that.

Proverb 2 DEFINE THE PROBLEM COMPLETELY

Good problem definitions are vital to the construction of good programs. An incomplete or ill-formed definition implies that the complete structure of the problem is not fully understood. Missing information, ignorance of special cases, and an abundance of extraneous information in a definition are good signs of poor programs, or at best, of programs that will be a surprise for the ultimate user. Any program that processes large amounts of data is bound to encounter some simple unnoticed condition, resulting in the all too common program crash.

We have often heard the claim that it is quite permissible to start with an imperfect problem definition, for during later program development a good programmer will readily pick up any critical points missed in the initial definition. We strongly disagree with this view. Starting with solid, complete (albeit laborious) problem definition is often half the solution to the entire problem. Moreover, good definitions can serve as the basis for good program documentation.

There are many reasons why good problem definitions are rare. First, there is no well-accepted idea of what comprises a good definition. Different programmers, instructors, and managers usually employ different definition techniques. For example, some project managers require only program narratives, decision tables, or system flowcharts. Another common practice is to have an experienced system analyst draw up several system flowcharts, some narrative descriptions, and some detailed descriptions of some inputs and outputs. Of course, the quality and completeness of these definitions will vary according to the style of the individual analyst.

Second, there is an almost irresistible temptation to skirt over the issue of definition in order to "get on with the job." This temptation is especially acute when the given problem is similar to previously solved problems or when there is strong external pressure to produce some quick, visible results (that is, programs). Furthermore, even if programmers could avoid the rush to get on with the job, management and the "customer" often make it difficult to invest the time and money in a good problem definition. The results of good definitions often appear to be wasted, since working code is usually delayed, especially when a programmer works hard to ensure that no problem situations go unnoticed.

Third, good problem definitions involve plain hard work. There is an intense amount of persistence and discipline required to get any definition straight.

As an example, consider the definition of Example 2.1a, which defines a program to aid a prospective homeowner in determining the financial arrangements of a mortgage loan. This definition is quite adequate, but on close analysis certain points need to be resolved. The formula that relates the values of the principal, interest rate, number of years, and monthly payment may not be readily available to the programmer. The formats for the input and output are not exactly clear, and several exceptional conditions that can arise in the computation are not mentioned. The definition of Example 2.1b resolves each of the above issues. It is a bit long but far more precise than that of Example 2.1a.

One important point of Example 2.1b is the inclusion of a sample of the input and output. Often a sample printout can be of great value to a programmer in giving a quick synopsis of the problem. In addition, a sample printout can often prevent surprises in cases where the program turns out to be quite different from the expectations of the person defining the problem. If a programmer is not given a sample of the input-output, he or she should try to provide a sample *before* programming.

In Chapter 3 we will discuss several ideas for producing good problem definitions in conjunction with a complete example. However, there are a few points about good definitions that deserve to be mentioned here. First, in attempting to supply a complete problem definition, the programmer probably cannot err by devoting a great deal of time and thought. While perfect definitions are probably unattainable, with good technique and discipline you will end up "close" to one. Remember that all languages have rigid rules for the execution of programs, and programmers must be specific to the last detail. If something is left unspecified in the original definition, the programmer will eventually have to face the consequences. At best, the changes that must be made are frustrating and distracting.

Once you believe that a definition is complete, put it aside for a time. Pick

Example 2.1 Proposed Definitions of a Mortgage Problem

Example 2.1a   Poor Problem Definition

We wish to devise a program to help potential homeowners assess the finances of mortgaging a home. There are four basic factors to be considered: the principal, the interest rate, the number of years for the mortgage, and the monthly payment. The program must input values for any three of the above quantities, output the fourth quantity, and also output a table indicating how the amount of the first monthly payment of each year is divided between principal and interest.

The input to this program is a line (or card) containing three of the above four figures:

Columns	Quantity
1–5	Principal
8–11	Interest rate
14–15	Number of years
18–22	Monthly payment

The principal and number of years are given as integers; the interest rate and monthly payments are given as fixed-point real numbers. The missing quantity is given as zero.

The output is to be a line indicating the value of the missing quantity, and a table giving, for the first monthly payment of each year, the amount contributed to decreasing the principal and the amount paid as interest.

Example 2.1b   Better Problem Definition

(1) *Problem Outline:*   We wish to devise a program to help potential homeowners assess the finances of mortgaging a home. There are four basic quantities to be considered:

P   The principal amount of the mortgage
I   The yearly interest rate for the mortgage
N   The number of years for the duration of the mortgage
M   The constant monthly payment required to pay back the principal P over N years at the interest rate I

The above quantities are related by the equation:

$$M = \frac{P * i * (1 + i)^n}{(i + i)^n - 1}$$

where

$i = I/12 =$ monthly interest rate
$n = 12*N =$ number of monthly periods in N years

Briefly, the program is to input any three of the above quantities, compute and print the fourth quantity, and also print a table specifying how the first monthly payment of each year is divided between interest and principal.

(2) *Input:*   The input to this program is a line (or card) of the form

column →	1	8	14	18
	↓	↓	↓	↓
	ddddd	d.dd	dd	ddd.dd
	P	I	N	M

where the d's represent decimal digits such that

P = the principal in dollars
I = the percentage interest rate computed to two decimal places
N = the number of years in integer form
M = the monthly payment in dollars and cents

The value of P, I, N, or M to be computed is given as zero. Except to the right of a decimal point, leading zeros may be replaced by blanks.

(3) *Output:*   The output from the program is to consist of two parts:
  (a) The value to be computed, using one of the formats:

PRINCIPAL   = $ddddd
INTEREST RATE   = d.dd
NUMBER OF YEARS   = dd
MONTHLY PAYMENT = $ddd.dd

  (b) A table giving for the first monthly payment of each year the amount paid to principal and the amount paid to interest. The headings and formats for the table values are as follows:

YEAR	AMT PAID TO PRINCIPAL	AMT PAID TO INTEREST
dd	$ddd.dd	$ddd.dd

Except to the right of a decimal point, leading zeros for any value are to be replaced by blanks.

(4) *Exceptional Conditions:*   If any of the input values are not in the prescribed format or if any output value is not in the range indicated, the program is to print an appropriate message to the user.

(5) *Sample Input:*

20000	8.00	22	0.00

(6) *Sample Output for Above Input:*

MONTHLY PAYMENT = $154.36

YEAR	AMT PAID TO PRINCIPAL	AMT PAID TO INTEREST
1	21.03	133.33
2	22.77	131.59
.		
.		
.		
25	142.53	11.83

it up later, and carefully reread and rethink it. Better still, have someone else read it (see Proverb 17). "Complete" problem definitions have been known to show flaws in the light of a new day. As a final word, make sure that you have a complete *written* description of the problem before you do anything else.

Proverb 3   START THE DOCUMENTATION EARLY

What can we say in one short proverb about a subject that has been discussed, written about, and cursed for years? Many have tried to define, motivate, and analyze good program documentation, the central purpose of which is to provide effective communication of factual information among people. The important thing is to do the documentation early. You will have a close touch with your user's or instructor's requirements; and most important, your understanding of the required program may be greatly enhanced.

On major programming projects, good documentation procedures share several characteristics:

1. *Readability is the chief goal.* Documentation is meant to be read by human beings. With good documentation, the reader does not have to stare at a shelf of material with no idea where to begin. The reader obtains exactly the information required, no more and no less.
2. *Documentation is based on good standards.* The what, when, and how of good documentation are recorded somewhere (i.e., standardized), and help is available to understand the standards.
3. *The required documentation is planned from the beginning.* Some documents are written long before others and serve as guides for the later ones. An efficient secretarial staff and automated aids help manage the load.
4. *Documentation is part of the daily programming process.* Finger-paralyzing treatises on long-forgotten topics are not needed. The documentation system drives the programming process!
5. *The procedures are carefully followed.* There is no pressure to skimp on documentation. Someone asks for needed documentation; someone reads it; and there is reward for producing high-quality documentation.

In all honesty, we must admit to finding few documentation systems as good as all this. It is possible to be involved in a programming project with a less than perfect documentation system. In this event, you should develop your own ideas and procedures early.

We all should be able to recognize good program documentation. The only thing left to do is to begin providing it. While you may not achieve a good documentation system right away, any step in that direction is to be preferred to the confusion that exists. Remember, however, to do it now, not later.

Proverb 4   THINK FIRST, CODE LATER

This proverb is intimately connected with the previous proverbs. After you have settled on the problem definition and its documentation procedures, the essential task is to start thinking about the solution as soon as possible, and to start the actual coding process only after you have devised a clear plan of attack.

Consider carefully the wording of this proverb: *Think first* means *think— do not code!* Start thinking while the problem is fresh in your mind and the deadline is as far away as it will ever be. Consider at least two different ways to solve the problem. Examine the approaches in sufficient detail to discover possible trouble spots or areas where the solution appears difficult. A top-notch program requires a top-notch algorithm.

Code later means *delay coding*. Give yourself some time to weed out difficult parts and polish the algorithm before trying to formalize it in actual code. It is much easier to discard poor thoughts than poor programs.

A common violation of this proverb lies in the approach to programming that we shall call the "linear" approach. In the linear approach, a programmer receives a problem and immediately starts preparing the code to solve it. Avoid this temptation, for it is full of hidden costs and dangers. You will certainly feel foolish continuously revising an ill-conceived program, or in the extreme case, writing a program that already exists on your system.

In conclusion, remember Murphy's second law of programming: It always takes longer to write a program than you think. A corollary might be: The sooner you start coding the program (instead of thinking about it), the longer it will take to finish the job.

Proverb 5   PROCEED TOP-DOWN

A major objective of this book is to advocate the "top-down" approach to programming problems. The top-down approach advocated here is not like conventional methods of programming. Furthermore, the top-down approach is itself subject to several interpretations, some of which overlook important issues. Top-down programming is discussed at length in Chapter 3. The following characteristics of the top-down approach are excerpts from that chapter.

1. *Design in Levels.* The programmer designs the program in *levels,* where a level consists of one or more modules. A module is always "complete," although it may reference unwritten submodules. The first level is a complete "main program." A lower level refines or develops unwritten modules in the upper level. In other words, the modules of a successive level consist of the submodules referenced in the prior level. The programmer may look several levels ahead to determine the best way to design the level at hand.

2. *Initial Language Independence.* The programmer initially uses expressions (often in English) that are relevant to the problem solution, even though the expressions cannot be directly transliterated into code. From statements that are machine and language independent, the programmer moves toward a final machine implementation in a programming language.

3. *Postponement of Details to Lower Levels.* The programmer concentrates on critical broad issues at the initial levels and postpones details (for example, choice of specific algorithms or intermediate data representations) until lower levels.

4. *Formalization of Each Level.* Before proceeding to a lower level, the programmer ensures that the "program" in its current stage of development is a "formal" statement. In most cases this means a program that calls unwritten submodules with all arguments spelled out. This step ensures that further sections of the program will be developed independently, without the need for subsequent changes in the specifications or the interfaces between modules.

5. *Verification of Each Level.* After generating the modules of a new level, the programmer verifies the developing formal statement of the program. This ensures that errors pertinent to the current level of development will be detected at their own level.

6. *Successive Refinements.* Each level of the program is refined, formalized, and verified in successive levels until the programmer obtains a complete program that can be transformed easily into code.

Consider Example 2.2, which gives the first level of the program for the programming problem of Chapter 3. Examining the definition of the problem, the programmer writes a complete but informal main program, P_1. After a somewhat more detailed look at the problem definition and considering the overall algorithm chosen earlier, the programmer develops P_1 into a formal version. The formal main program is in some sense complete and can be verified as if it had been written in an actual programming language. The code to produce the modules referenced in P_1 must be developed in P_2 and further refined in successive levels.

Top-down programming has two distinct advantages. First, a programmer is initially freed from the confines of a particular language and can deal with more natural data structures or actions. Second, it leads to a modular approach that allows the programmer to write statements relevant to the current structures or actions. The details can be developed later in separate modules. In fact, the

Example 2.2   Initial Steps in the Top-Down Approach

P_1 *(First pass)*

    initialize program variables
10   get a proposed move

    if move is not legal
      then goto 10
      else process the move

    if the game is not over
      then change players and *goto* 10

    end the game and stop

P_1 *(Formal)*

    gosub INITIALIZE(PLAYER,BOARD)
    write (INTRODUCTORY-MESSAGES)

10   input (MOVE) from PLAYER

    if MOVE is not on board
      then goto 10

    if NOT LEGAL-MOVE(PLAYER,BOARD,MOVE)
      then write (ILLEGAL-MOVE-MSG)
        goto 10

    gosub UPDATE-BOARD(PLAYER,BOARD,MOVE)
    if LEGAL-JUMP(PLAYER,BOARD,MOVE) and
      JUMP-CAN-BE-CONTINUED(PLAYER,BOARD,MOVE)
      then gosub CONTINUE-THE-JUMP(PLAYER,BOARD,MOVE)

    if NO-KING(BOARD,PLAYER) and MOVES-LEFT(BOARD,OPPONENT)
      then swap PLAYERS
        inform (PLAYER) of completed move
        prompt (OPPONENT) for next move
        goto 10

    write (WINNING-MSG) for PLAYER,
        (LOSING-MSG) for OPPONENT
  stop

main goal of top-down programming is just that: to aid the programmer in writing well-structured, modular programs.

We cannot really say it all here. Chapter 3 tells the whole story.

Proverb 6 BEWARE OF OTHER APPROACHES

Traditionally, programmers have used many different approaches to a program. Consider the following list:

1. Bottom-up approach
2. Inside-out or forest approach
3. Linear approach
4. Typical systems analyst approach
5. Imitation approach

In the "bottom-up" approach, the programmer writes the lower modules first and the upper levels later. The bottom-up approach is in a sense the inversion of the top-down approach. It suffers severely by requiring the programmer to make specific decisions about the program before the overall problem and algorithm are understood.

In between the top-down and the bottom-up approaches, we have the "inside-out" or "forest" approach, which consists of starting in the middle of the program and working down and up at the same time. Roughly speaking, it goes as follows:

1. *General Idea*. First we decide upon the general idea for programming the problem.
2. *A Rough Sketch of the Program*. Next we write any "important" sections of the program, assuming initialization in some form. In some sections we write portions of the actual code. In doing this, we hope that the actual intent of each piece of code will not change several times, necessitating rewriting parts of our sketch.
3. *Coding the First Version*. After Step 2, we write specific code for the entire program. We start with the lowest level module. After an individual module has been coded, we debug it and immediately prepare a description of what it does.
4. *Rethinking and Revising*. As a result of Step 3, we should be close to a working program, but it may be possible to improve on it. So we continue by making several improvements until we obtain a complete working program.

We think it fair to say that many programmers often work inside out. Usually they don't start very close to the top or bottom levels. Instead they start in the middle and work outward until a program finally appears on the horizon. The approach is a poor one, for the program may undergo many changes and patches and thus seldom achieves a clear logical structure.

The third method is called the "linear" approach. Here, one immediately starts writing code as it will appear when executed: first line first, second line second, and so forth. The debit with this approach is the need to make specific detailed decisions with very little assurance that they are appropriate to the problem at hand. One must then accept the consequences. This technique may seem obviously poor, but the temptation to use it can be strong, especially on "easy" programs. Beware of this temptation, for there is no such thing as an easy program.

The fourth technique is the typical "systems analyst" approach. When used wisely it can be an effective technique, and admittedly it has been successfully used for many large programs. We shall briefly compare it with the top-down approach, the technique advocated in this book.

The systems analyst often starts on a large programming problem by dividing up the task on the basis of the flow of control he sees in the overall program. The flowchart picturing the flow is broken into a number of modules, which are then farmed out to the programmers. After these have been completed, the analyst will firm up the interfaces and try to make things work right. The lower level modules receive attention before their function and data requirements are explicit. The resulting program modules are primarily determined by the flow of control through the program; thus the importance of flowcharts with this technique.

With the top-down approach, on the other hand, the flow of control is subservient to the logical structure. There does not have to be an identifiable flow of control that is easy to flowchart. The flow of control is rather like traversing a tree. It starts at the top level, goes down one or more levels, comes back, goes on to another level, and so forth. The top-down approach thus has little need for flowcharting.

As a final method, consider what we call the "imitation" approach, a method superficially resembling the top-down approach. This approach is discussed in detail because many programmers *think* that the top-down approach is really the way they have always programmed. We claim that there are often subtle but important differences. The imitation approach is described as follows:

1. *Thinking about the Program.* Having been given a programming assignment, take the time to examine the problem thoroughly before starting to program. Think about the details of the program for a while, and then decide on a general approach.

2. *Deciding on Submodules.* After having thought about the problem in detail, decide on what sections will be sufficiently important to merit being made into submodules.

3. *Data Representation.* After compiling a list of the submodules, decide on a data representation that will enable them to be efficient, unless the representation is already specified.

4. *Coding of Submodules.* At this point write each submodule. After each is completed, write down what it expects as input, what it returns as output, and what it does. The submodules should be written in a hierarchical manner: the most primitive first, calling routines second, and so forth.

Doing this will ensure that the submodules are fully coded before the upper-level program structures are finalized.

5. *Coding the Main Program.* After all submodules have been written, write the main program. The purpose of the main program will be sequencing and interfacing the subroutines.

The imitation approach has some important resemblances to the top-down approach:

1. The programmer must understand the problem thoroughly before writing code.
2. The actual writing of the program is postponed until after certain decisions have been made.
3. The problem is broken up into logical units.

However, there are important different characteristics in the two approaches.

1. In the top-down approach, a *specific* plan of attack is developed in stages. Only the issues relevant to a given level are considered, and these issues are formalized completely.
2. Furthermore, whenever the programmer decides to use a subprogram or procedure, the interfaces (i.e., arguments, returned values, and effects) are decided *first*. The inputs and outputs are formalized before developing the submodule; that is, the submodules are made to fit the calling routine instead of the other way around.
3. Most important, at *every step* in the top-down approach, the programmer must have a complete, correct "program."

The major disadvantages of the imitation approach are that it is more likely to produce errors, to require major program modifications, or to result in a somewhat ill-conceived program. Choosing a partially specified attack may require serious changes to the program. Coding submodules first may result in a confusing program logic if the submodules do not happen to integrate easily into the upper level code designed later.

In summary, think carefully about programming technique. The top-down approach, which is discussed at length in Chapter 3, may provide a wise alternative.

Proverb 7   CODE IN LOGICAL UNITS

The best programs are those that can be understood easily. There are no superfluous details and the logical structure is clear. Such well-structured programs are always a by-product of a careful development process and are usually characterized by small, functionally specific modules. Generally, the statements of a BASIC module should not extend beyond one page.

The most direct value of modular code is felt during program maintenance,

2.1a Poor Logical Structure   2.1b Better Logical Structure

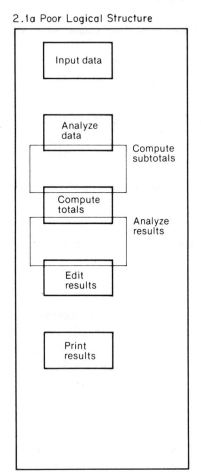

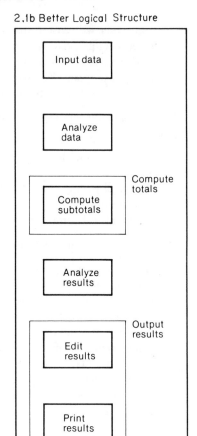

Fig. 2.1   Display of logical structure

for time is not wasted trying to determine what is being done over several sections of code. Consider Fig. 2.1a, which outlines the logical structure of a hypothetical program. The structure is difficult to follow. Figure 2.1b pictures the remedied situation where simple computations are isolated in units.

There are many assets to modular code. Coding time is shortened by the use of previously written modules. Implementation costs are lower because of easier overlaying, decreased recompilation costs, smaller tasks, and isolated code bottlenecks. Testing is much simpler because of the fact that "simple" modules usually have no more than, say, a half dozen looping and branching constructs and thus a small number of total execution paths.

When the time comes to write actual code, there are three guidelines that will help you code in logical units:

1. First and most obviously, make good use of functions and subroutines.
2. Avoid confusing control structures.
3. Display the resulting logical structure with good spacing and indentation.

The next three proverbs treat these issues.

Proverb 8 USE FUNCTIONS AND SUBROUTINES

The function and subroutine facilities in BASIC can be powerful tools for coding clear, modular programs. Not only do these facilities allow the programmer to "factor out" frequently executed sections of code, but more important, they provide a basic unit for abstraction of program modules. This abstraction can have a great effect on program readability by exposing the program's logical structure, *even if* the function or subroutine is called only once.

Consider the programs of Example 2.3. Given the values for the three-element arrays A, B, C, and D, the programs use the determinant method—assuming D$\emptyset$ (denominator) is nonzero—to solve three independent equations of the following form for the unknowns x, y, and z:

$$A_1 x + B_1 y + C_1 z = D_1$$
$$A_2 x + B_2 y + C_2 z = D_2$$
$$A_3 x + B_3 y + C_3 z = D_3$$

The program of Example 2.3a is a confusion of arithmetic calculations. It

Example 2.3 Solution of Three Independent Equations

EXAMPLE 2.3A   POOR SOLUTION WITHOUT USING FUNCTIONS

```
100          DIM A(3), B(3), C(3), D(3)
110 REM
120          MAT INPUT A, B, C, D
130 REM
140          LET D1 = (A(1)*B(2)*C(3)) + (A(2)*B(3)*C(1)) + (A(3)*B(1)*C(2))
150          LET D2 = (A(3)*B(2)*C(1)) + (A(2)*B(1)*C(3)) + (A(1)*B(3)*C(2))
160          LET D0 = D1 - D2
170          LET X1 = (D(1)*B(2)*C(3)) + (D(2)*B(3)*C(1)) + (D(3)*B(1)*C(2))
180          LET X2 = (D(3)*B(2)*C(1)) + (D(2)*B(1)*C(3)) + (D(1)*B(3)*C(2))
190          LET X  = X1 - X2
200          LET Y1 = (A(1)*D(2)*C(3)) + (A(2)*D(3)*C(1)) + (A(3)*D(1)*C(2))
210          LET Y2 = (A(3)*D(2)*C(1)) + (A(2)*D(1)*C(3)) + (A(1)*D(3)*C(2))
220          LET Y  = Y1 - Y2
230          LET Z1 = (A(1)*B(2)*D(3)) + (A(2)*B(3)*D(1)) + (A(3)*B(1)*D(2))
240          LET Z2 = (A(3)*B(2)*D(1)) + (A(2)*B(1)*D(3)) + (A(1)*B(3)*D(2))
250          LET Z  = Z1 - Z2
260 REM
270          LET X  = X / D0
280          LET Y  = Y / D0
290          LET Z  = Z / D0
300 REM
310          PRINT 'X = '; X, 'Y = '; Y, 'Z = '; Z
320 REM
330 REM
340          END
```

Example 2.3 Solution of Three Independent Equations (Cont'd)

EXAMPLE 2.3B   BETTER SOLUTION USING A FUNCTION SUBPROGRAM

```
100         DIM A(3), B(3), C(3), D(3)
110 REM
120             MAT INPUT A, B, C, D
130 REM
140             LET D0 = FND(A(1),B(1),C(1),A(2),B(2),C(3),A(3),B(3),C(3))
150             LET X  = FND(D(1),B(1),C(1),D(2),B(2),C(2),D(3),B(3),C(3))
160             LET Y  = FND(A(1),D(1),C(1),A(2),D(2),C(2),A(3),D(3),C(3))
170             LET Z  = FND(A(1),B(1),D(1),A(2),B(2),D(2),A(3),B(3),D(3))
180 REM
190             LET X  = X / D0
200             LET Y  = Y / D0
210             LET Z  = Z / D0
220 REM
230             PRINT 'X = '; X,  'Y = '; Y,  'Z = '; Z
240 REM
250 REM
260         END
```

```
100         DEF FND (X1, X2, X3, Y1, Y2, Y3, Z1, Z2, Z3)
110 REM
120 REM
130             LET FND =   (X1*Y2*Z3) + (X2*Y3*Z1) + (X3*Y1*Z2)
140             LET FND = - (X3*Y2*Z1) + (X2*Y1*Z3) + (X1*Y3*Z2) + FND
150 REM
160 REM
170         FNEND
```

EXAMPLE 2.3C   STILL BETTER SOLUTION USING A FUNCTION
SUBPROGRAM AND PASSING ARRAYS AS ARGUMENTS

```
100         DIM A(3), B(3), C(3), D(3)
110 REM
120             MAT INPUT A, B, C, D
130 REM
140             LET D0 = FND (A, B, C)
150             LET X  = FND (D, B, C) / D0
160             LET Y  = FND (A, D, C) / D0
170             LET Z  = FND (A, B, D) / D0
180 REM
190             PRINT 'X = '; X,  'Y = '; Y,  'Z = '; Z
200 REM
210 REM
220         END
```

```
100         DEF FND (R, S, T)
110 REM
120         DIM R(3), S(3), T(3)
130 REM
140 REM
150             LET F1 = (R(1)*S(2)*T(3)) + (R(2)*S(3)*T(1)) + (R(3)*S(1)*T(2))
160             LET F2 = (R(3)*S(2)*T(1)) + (R(2)*S(1)*T(3)) + (R(1)*S(3)*T(2))
170 REM
180             LET FND = F1 - F2
190 REM
200 REM
210         FNEND
```

contains little hint of the determinant method or the algorithm needed to solve the problem. In contrast, Example 2.3b uses a function subprogram to calculate the determinants. It is explicitly clear that each unknown is the quotient of two determinants and that the denominator is the determinant of the variable coefficient matrix. Example 2.3c shows an even greater improvement when the arrays are passed as arguments, a feature which is not in standard BASIC.

In brief, use functions and subroutines *often*. Even if your program is longer as a result, they can make it more structured and easier to understand.

Proverb 9   WATCH OUT FOR GOTOs

Over the past ten years, one programming issue has been the subject of more papers, more opinions, and more controversy than any other: control structures. The control structures for specifying the flow of control in a program are indeed important. At every point in a program the next action to be carried out must be specified. In many languages, and in BASIC particularly, the control structure issue focuses on one small statement—the GOTO.

The unconditional transfer of control, which is the function of the GOTO statement, has been associated with programming since its inception. Its historical ties have left indelible marks on today's major programming languages. Until recently, virtually all higher level languages have had some form of an unrestricted GOTO. Yet, of all the linguistic constructs in today's languages, few have been debated more often or more intensively. The GOTO is not intrinsically evil, but its abuses can be avoided by using more transparent linguistic features and by using the GOTO in a highly controlled manner.

Our fundamental position is to permit only those control structures for which the programmer can develop a ''static'' assessment of a program or program fragment. Chapter 4 gives a list of the control structures that we believe are sufficient for wisely handling the control structure problem in BASIC. For the rest of this proverb, we will concentrate on the major culprit, the GOTO.

Consider first the very simple Examples 2.4 and 2.5, and notice the elimination of GOTOs in favor of FOR loops, IF statements, and built-in functions. With their removal, a clearer structure arises, and the program shortens.

In a more realistic setting, consider the two programs of Example 2.6. Here we see simple subroutines for finding an occurrence of a substring (designated by two character positions) in a given target string. Under certain conditions, the subroutine sets an error flag. In Example 2.6a, we see a quite tightly nested series of interconnected transfers of control. The next example, 2.6b, is a program derived from the use of alternative control structures. The second example provides a much clearer description of the algorithm, mainly because of the use of simple 1-in, 1-out control structures.

The differences between these two programs are quite clearly expressed in their corresponding flowcharts, shown in Figs. 2.2 and 2.3. In Fig. 2.3, the

Example 2.4 Elimination of GOTOs in Favor of FOR-Loops

EXAMPLE 2.4A   POOR

```
100 REM
110 REM    **   LOCAL VARIABLES
120 REM    **   S...SUM
130 REM    **   C...COUNT
140 REM    **   M...MAXIMUM INTEGER
150 REM
160        DATA 100
170 REM
180            READ M
190            LET S = 0
200            LET C = 0
210            IF (C > M)   GOTO 260
220                LET S = S + C
230                LET C = C + 1
240                GOTO 210
250 REM
260            PRINT 'SUM = ', S
270 REM
280        END
```

EXAMPLE 2.4B   BETTER

```
100        DATA 100
110 REM
120            READ M
130            LET S = 0
140 REM
150            FOR C = 1 TO M
160                S = S + C
170            NEXT C
180 REM
190            PRINT 'SUM = ', S
200 REM
210        END
```

Example 2.5 Elimination of GOTOs in Favor of IF Statements and Built-In Functions

EXAMPLE 2.5A   POOR

```
100        IF (A > B)   GOTO 130
110            LET D = B - A
120            GOTO 140
130        LET D = A - B
140        PRINT D
```

EXAMPLE 2.5B   BETTER

```
100        LET D = A - B
110        IF (D < 0)   D = -D
120        PRINT D
```

EXAMPLE 2.5C   BEST

```
100        D = ABS(A-B)
110        PRINT D
```

Example 2.6 Control Structures

EXAMPLE 2.6A   POOR

```
100 REM    **   SUBROUTINE TO EXTRACT A SUBSTRING
110 REM
120 REM    **   INPUT VARIABLES -
130 REM    **      S  - SOURCE STRING
140 REM    **      N  - NUMBER OF CHARACTERS IN SOURCE STRING
150 REM    **      F  - FIRST CHARACTER LOCATION
160 REM    **      L  - LAST CHARACTER LOCATION
170 REM
180 REM    **   OUTPUT VARIABLES -
190 REM    **      S1 - SUBSTRING
200 REM    **      N1 - NUMBER OF CHARACTERS IN SUBSTRING
210 REM    **      E  - ERROR FLAG
220 REM
230 REM
240            DIM S(80), S1(80)
250            DATA 80
260 REM
270               READ M
280 REM
290               IF (F-1  < 0)   GOTO 310
300               IF (F-1 >= 0)   GOTO 350
310                  LET E$ = 'TRUE'
320                  GOTO 500
330 REM
340 REM
350               IF (L-1  < 0)   GOTO 310
360               IF (L-1 >= 0)   GOTO 370
370                  LET N1 = (L - F) + 1
380                  IF (N-N1  < 0)   GOTO 310
390                  IF (N-N1 >= 0)   GOTO 400
400                  IF (N1-M >= 0)   GOTO 310
410                  IF (N1-M  < 0)   GOTO 440
420 REM
430 REM
440                  FOR I = F TO L
450                     LET J = (I - F) + 1
460                     LET S1$(J) = S$(I)
470                  NEXT I
480 REM
490 REM
500            RETURN
```

EXAMPLE 2.6B   BETTER

```
100 REM    **   SUBROUTINE TO EXTRACT A SUBSTRING
110 REM
120 REM    **   INPUT VARIABLES -
130 REM    **      S  - SOURCE STRING
140 REM    **      N  - NUMBER OF CHARACTERS IN SOURCE STRING
150 REM    **      F  - FIRST CHARACTER LOCATION
160 REM    **      L  - LAST CHARACTER LOCATION
170 REM
180 REM    **   OUTPUT VARIABLES -
190 REM    **      S1 - SUBSTRING
200 REM    **      N1 - NUMBER OF CHARACTERS IN SUBSTRING
210 REM    **      E  - ERROR FLAG
220 REM
230 REM
240            DIM S(80), S1(80)
250            DATA 80
260 REM
270               READ M
```

Example 2.6 Control Structures (Cont'd.)

```
280 REM
290             LET E$ = 'TRUE'
300 REM
310             IF (F <= 0)  GOTO 480
320             IF (L <= 0) . GOTO 480
330 REM
340 REM
350               LET N1 = (L - F) + 1
360               IF (N1 > N)   GOTO 480
370               IF (N1 > M)   GOTO 480
380 REM
390 REM
400                 FOR I = F TO L
410                   LET J = (I - F) + 1
420                   LET S1$(J) = S$(I)
430                 NEXT I
440 REM
450                 LET E$ = 'FALSE'
460 REM
470 REM
480         RETURN
```

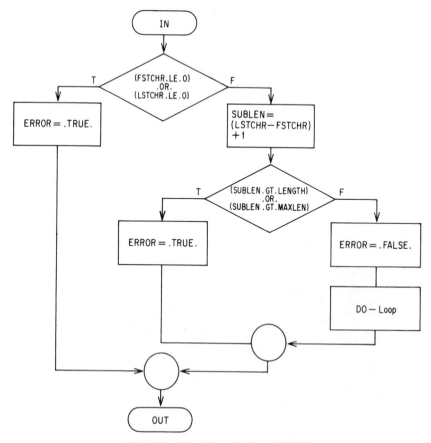

Fig. 2.2   Flowchart for Example 2.6b

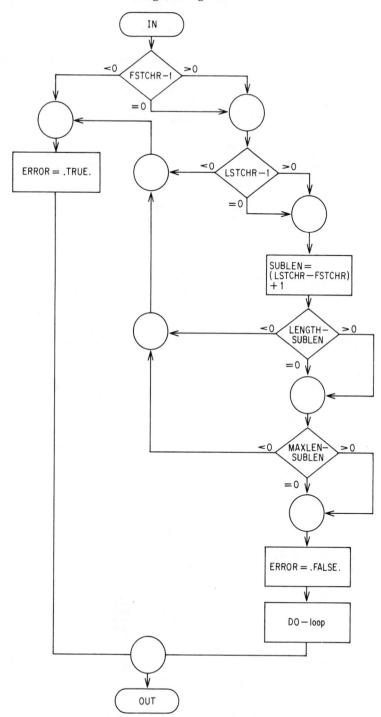

Fig. 2.3 Flowchart for Example 2.6a

flowchart shows a profusion of branching lines; in Fig. 2.2, on the other hand, a clearer structure is evident.

In another setting, consider the program segments of Example 2.7. These

Example 2.7 A Variant of the Bubble Sort Algorithm

EXAMPLE 2.7A   POOR

```
100         DIM A(500)
110         DATA 500
120 REM
130 REM
140             READ L
150             LET J = 1
160             IF (J = L) GOTO 360
170                 IF (A(J) <= A(J+1))  GOTO 320
180                     LET T       = A(J)
190                     LET A(J)    = A(J+1)
200                     LET A(J+1) = T
210 REM
220                     LET K = J
230                     LET K = K - 1
240                     IF (K = 0)  GOTO 320
250                     IF (A(K) <= A(K+1))  GOTO 230
260                         LET T       = A(K)
270                         LET A(K)    = A(K+1)
280                         LET A(K+1) = T
290                         GOTO 230
300 REM
310 REM
320                 LET J = J + 1
330                 GOTO 160
340 REM
350 REM
360             MAT PRINT A
370 REM
380 REM
390         END
```

EXAMPLE 2.7B   BETTER

```
100         DIM A(500)
110         DATA 500
120 REM
130 REM
140             READ L
150 REM
160             FOR J = 1 TO L
170                 IF (A(J) <= A(J+1))  GOTO 280
180                     LET T       = A(J)
190                     LET A(J)    = A(J+1)
200                     LET A(J+1) = T
210 REM
220                     FOR K = J-1 TO 1 STEP -1
230                         IF (A(K) <= A(K+1))  GOTO 270
240                             LET T       = A(K)
250                             LET A(K)    = A(K+1)
260                             LET A(K+1) = T
270                     NEXT K
280             NEXT J
290 REM
300 REM
310             MAT PRINT A
320 REM
330 REM
340         END
```

segments employ a variation of the bubble sort algorithm to sort an array A, containing 500 entries. Basically, the programs scan the array A once from the top (position 1) to the bottom (position 500). At each examined position in the array, the elements at the top of the position are already in order, and the program checks to see if the element in the next position is itself in order. If not, the element is swapped with the previous element and then "bubbled" up until its proper place in the sorted part of the array is found. Processing then continues at the position below the element originally examined.

The BASIC program of Example 2.7a is oriented towards the efficient use of the GOTO statement. The resulting program is somewhat difficult to understand. The program of Example 2.7b avoids unnecessary use of GOTO.

One major point of this example is that the (possibly) small gain in efficiency via the GOTO is not as important as the improvement in clarity when the programmer uses alternative ways of constructing his program.

In summary, the deeper issue here is not merely the elimination of GOTOs but the use of a clear, logical program structure. The trouble with GOTOs is that when they are abused, they can lead a programmer down the path of a confusing, almost spaghetti-like, logic. Chapter 4, which discusses program standards, provides specific rules that limit the use of GOTOs to well-formed control structures. If you stick to these standards *from the beginning,* the GOTO problem will be diminished.

Proverb 10   PRETTYPRINT

If there is one proverb that is simple to follow but enormously effective, this is it. Briefly stated, "prettyprinting" is the effective utilization of "extra" spaces, blank lines, or special characters to illuminate the logical structure of a program.

Prettyprinting is especially important in the verification and maintenance of programs. With good prettyprinting it is fairly easy to detect errors, such as improperly structured data description entries and incorrectly nested IF statements. Furthermore, a programmer trying to read the program does not have to devote extra time to discovering its structure, an advantage that makes it considerably easier to understand.

Some implementations of BASIC allow a generous use of blank spaces and lines to promote prettyprinting. As an example, two complete programs are listed in Examples 2.8a and 2.8b. The first is not well prettyprinted; the second shows careful thought in prettyprinting. Most textbooks do not expose users to the full possibilities of prettyprinting, although almost every implementation admits great latitude in the spacing of programs.

There is one especially important point—the use of blank REM lines. The blank line is excellent for separating modules of the program and highlighting critical sections. Examine prettyprinted Example 2.8b. Note how logical sections of the program become apparent solely because of the use of blank lines.

Example 2.8 Prettyprinting

EXAMPLE 2.8A   POOR

```
100 REM VOWEL COUNT ALGORITHM
110 DATA 'A', 'E', 'I', 'O', 'U', 'STOP'
120 READ A$, E$, I$, O$, U$, S$
130       LET A1=0
140       LET E1=0
150       LET I1=0
160       LET O1=0
170       LET U1=0
180 REM COUNT VOWELS UNTIL 'STOP' IS INPUT
190       INPUT X$
200       IF(X$=S$)GOTO 360
210       IF(X$<>A$)GOTO 240
220       LET A1=A1+1
230       GOTO 190
240       IF(X$<>E$)GOTO 270
250       LET E1=E1+1
260       GOTO 190
270       IF(X$<>I$ )GOTO 300
280       LET I1=I1+1
290       GOTO 190
300       IF(X$<>O$)GOTO 330
310       LET O1=O1+1
320       GOTO 190
330       IF(X$<>U$)GOTO 190
340       LET U1=U1+1
350       GOTO 190
360       PRINT '#A=',A1,'#E=',E1,'#I=',I1,'#O=',O1,'#U=',U1
370       END
```

EXAMPLE 2.8B   GOOD PRETTYPRINTING

```
100 REM   ** VOWEL COUNT ALGORITHM
110 REM
120 REM
130       DATA 'A', 'E', 'I', 'O', 'U', 'STOP'
140 REM
150           READ A$, E$, I$, O$, U$, S$
160 REM
170           LET A1 = 0
180           LET E1 = 0
190           LET I1 = 0
200           LET O1 = 0
210           LET U1 = 0
220 REM
230 REM   ** COUNT VOWELS UNTIL 'STOP' IS INPUT
240 REM
250           INPUT X$
260 REM
270       IF (X$ = S$) GOTO 460
280 REM
290               IF (X$ <> A$) GOTO 320
300               LET A1 = A1+1
310               GOTO 250
320               IF (X$ <> E$) GOTO 350
330               LET E1 = E1+1
340               GOTO 250
350               IF (X$ <> I$) GOTO 380
360               LET I1 = I1+1
370               GOTO 250
380               IF (X$ <> O$) GOTO 410
390               LET O1 = O1+1
400               GOTO 250
410               IF (X$ <> U$) GOTO 250
420               LET U1 = U1+1
430               GOTO 250
```

88526

Example 2.8 Prettyprinting (Cont'd.)

```
440  REM
450  REM
460        PRINT 'VOWEL COUNT RESULTS'
470        PRINT '_____'
480        PRINT
490        PRINT ' A = ', A1
500        PRINT ' E = ', E1
510        PRINT ' I = ', I1
520        PRINT ' O = ', O1
530        PRINT ' U = ', U1
540        END
```

Unfortunately, some implementations remove the extra spaces typed by the user and thus make prettyprinting almost impossible. We strongly object to such implementations. One way to beat this problem is to use colored pencils and a straightedge to bracket pieces of code.

In all our examples, we have attempted to incorporate certain prettyprinting standards. Appendix B itemizes most of these standards; they are the product of many revisions and should be useful to all BASIC programmers. We encourage the reader to make use of additional prettyprinting standards as they are discovered. But do not hesitate to use the standards as they appear. If the program you are writing has a good logical structure, then show it!

Proverb 11 COMMENT EFFECTIVELY

Comments are a form of internal documentation that allows the programmer to describe the internal workings of a program. It must be admitted that the BASIC comment convention is inconvenient. One must use an entire new line for a comment that might be more informative if placed within or at the end of a statement line. Nevertheless, comments are invaluable for illuminating the logical structure of a program and as reference points for making documentation.

One example will suffice to make the point. Consider the program of Example 2.9a. This program represents the ultimate in obscurity, a program with no comments. The reader is invited to examine the program and determine the meaning of each statement.

Next consider the program of Example 2.9b. The comments convey the logical structure of the program. This information is particularly valuable to someone who is using the program without a copy of the documentation or to someone who doesn't want to spend any excess time trying to figure out the program.

The comments in Example 2.9b, however, are not optimal. Example 2.9c shows a deeper concern for the reader. The comments are clearly separated from the code and give more precise statements about the entire function, even telling us about Euclid's algorithms.

Although the value of using comments can be illustrated over and over again, the programmer is often tempted not to use them. After all, when a

MERNER-PFEIFFER LIBRARY
TENNESSEE WESLEYAN COLLEGE

Example 2.9 Use of Effective Comments

EXAMPLE 2.9A   POOR...NO COMMENTS

```
100        DEF FNG (F, S)
110           LET R = S
120           LET Q = F / R
130           LET R = F - (Q * R)
140           IF (R = 0)   GOTO 170
150           LET FNG = R
160           GOTO 120
170        FNEND
```

EXAMPLE 2.9B   BETTER...PAYING TOKEN REGARD TO GOOD COMMENTING

```
100        DEF FNG (F, S)
110 REM
120 REM    **   FUNCTION TO COMPUTE THE GREATEST COMMON DIVISOR
130 REM    **   OF TWO NUMBERS USING EUCLID'S ALGORITHM
140 REM
150 REM    ** USING  - FIRST NUMBER, SECOND NUMBER
160 REM    ** GIVING - GREATEST COMMON DIVISOR OF BOTH NUMBERS
170 REM
180           LET R = S
190           LET Q = F / R
200           LET R = F - (Q * R)
210 REM
220           IF (R = 0)   GOTO 270
230              LET FNG = R
240              GOTO 190
250 REM
260 REM
270        FNEND
```

EXAMPLE 2.9C   BEST...CAREFUL COMMENTING

```
100        DEF FNG (F, S)
110 REM
120 REM    **   ABSTRACT-
130 REM    **      EUCLID'S ALGORITHM FOR COMPUTING A GREATEST
140 REM    **      COMMON DIVISOR.  MULTIPLES OF THE QUOTIENT
150 REM    **      OF THE TWO INPUT NUMBERS ARE SUBTRACTED UNTIL
160 REM    **      THE REMAINDER EQUALS ZERO.
170 REM
180 REM    ** USING  - FIRST NUMBER, SECOND NUMBER
190 REM
200 REM    ** GIVING - GREATEST COMMON DIVISOR OF BOTH NUMBERS
210 REM
220           LET R = S
230 REM
240           LET Q = F / S
250           LET R = F - (Q * R)
260 REM
270           IF (R = 0)   GOTO 330
280 REM
290           LET FNG = R
300           GOTO 240
310 REM
320 REM
330        FNEND
```

---

programmer is writing a piece of code, comments may not be needed. But how many times during coding does the programmer go back to try to figure out what has happened and what is left to do? And what about the next day? Or the next week? Or the occasion when you are asked to change someone else's program?

One additional proverb is useful here: *Temperance is moderation in all things*. Comments can be overused as well as misused. It is far better to use good prettyprinting rather than to clutter up your code with copious comments. Comments should convey useful information. Frequent comments like

REM   ** A GETS B PLUS C
LET A = B + C

not only clutter up your program but may completely discourage anyone from trying to wade through it. In short, comments can promote the design of truly maintainable programs. They can really make a difference. *Use them, temperately.*

Proverb 12   GET THE SYNTAX CORRECT NOW

How many times have you heard the BASIC language being roundly cursed for its highly sensitive syntax or a BASIC interpreter compiler being criticized for not helping to add "trivial" missing spaces or commas?

Consider the program fragments of Example 2.10a, which contain such trivial syntactic errors. Example 2.10b shows the corresponding corrected versions. (Note: In implementations that relax some of the requirements of standard BASIC, some of the constructs in Example 2.10a may be legal.) Errors like the

Example 2.10 Some Simple Syntactic Errors

```
               EXAMPLE 2.10A   WRONG

     (1)    FOR I = 1, 10

     (2)    GOTO 100

     (3)    IF (CAT = DOG)    GOTO 10

     (4)    LET X = 'NO DOLLAR SIGN'

     (5)    X = Y

     (6)    GOSUB SORT

     (7)    IF ((X = Y) AND (A = B) GOTO 100

     (8)    DATA X / 3.0 /

     (9)    DIM A(3,3)
            LET A(5)  = 0

     (10)   FUNCTION FNA (A, B)
```

Example 2.10 Some Simple Syntactic Errors (Cont'd.)

EXAMPLE 2.10B   CORRECT

(1)   FOR I = 1 TO 10

(2)   GOTO 100

(3)   IF (C = D)   GOTO 10

(4)   LET X$ = 'NO DOLLAR SIGN'

(5)   LET X = Y

(6)   GOSUB 100

(7)   IF ((X = Y) AND (A = B)) GOTO 100

(8)   DATA 3.0
       READ X

(9)   DIM A(3,3)
       LET A(2,2)   = 0

(10)   DEF FNA (A, B)

---

ones in the first example should be screened out in advance by a careful programmer. It is our contention that no errors, no matter how trivial, should pass the attention of a good programmer, for it is possible that some of them may not be detected by the compiler and will appear only after a program is in full operation.

Furthermore, there is little excuse for syntactic errors in programs, since the manual specifies the syntax for you. The time to consider syntax is not while verifying the completed program but while preparing it. Keep the manual or composite language skeleton handy as you write the code, and if you are not absolutely positive that the syntax of the statement you are writing is perfect, look it up. It only takes a few seconds, and your grasp of the language will increase with constant references to the manual. This work habit is all the more crucial if you are just learning BASIC or if you have done considerable programming in another language with similar but nevertheless different syntactic constructs.

You can and should write programs that are completely free of syntactic errors on the first run. We mean it. But to do so, you first must convince yourself that indeed you can do it. Second, *you must get someone else to read the work you produce* (see Proverb 17). Just think of all the hours of turn-around time you can waste tracking down simple syntactic errors, not to mention some severe run-time problems that can be caused by ''trivial'' errors.

Proverb 13   DON'T LEAVE THE READER IN THE DUST

Every programmer has a secret desire to produce a truly clever program. Shortening the code, running the program faster, or using fewer variables are all popular pastimes. Resist this temptation because the benefits seldom match the hidden costs. A good programmer writes code that is simple to read and quick to the point.

Consider Example 2.11. Each element of code is designed to select the player leading the first card in a card game. Successively higher bids are represented by successively increasing integers. The four-element integer array B (Bid) contains the final bids by each of the four players. The players are numbered clockwise from one to four, and the lead player is the person to the left of the highest bidder. Notice that Example 2.11a eliminates several lines of code. Would you use it in your card-playing program?

If you do prefer the program of 2.11a to that of 2.11b, look at both examples carefully. Do you prefer the first because it executes more rapidly or requires less storage? On the computer you regularly use, you may in fact find that Example 2.11b requires less storage, because the loop may take fewer instructions than the straightline code from the corresponding statement in 2.11a. In addition, Example 2.11b may execute faster because no divisions or multiplications are required, and there may be fewer additions. In short, beware of "clever" code, and beware of being penny-wise but pound-foolish.

Example 2.11 Code to Determine Leading Player

```
          EXAMPLE 2.11A   TRICKY VERSION

100 REM
110 REM   **   NOTE USE OF SYSTEM-SUPPLIED MOD FUNCTION
120       DIM B(4)
130 REM
140           LET N = (B(1)/M) + 2*(B(2)/M) + 3*(B(3)/M) + 4*(B(4)/M)
150           LET L = 1 + FNM (N, 4)
160 REM
170           PRINT 'THE LEADER IS PLAYER NUMBER ', L
180 REM
190 REM
200       END



          EXAMPLE 2.11B   NATURAL VERSION

100       DIM B(4)
110       DATA 4
120 REM
130 REM
140           READ N
150 REM
160           FOR P = 1 TO N
170               IF (B(P) <> M) GOTO 190
180                   LET B1 = P
190           NEXT P
200 REM
210           LET L = 1
220           IF (B1 = N)   GOTO 250
230               LET L = P + 1
240 REM
250           PRINT 'THE LEADER IS PLAYER NUMBER', L
260 REM
270 REM
280       END
```

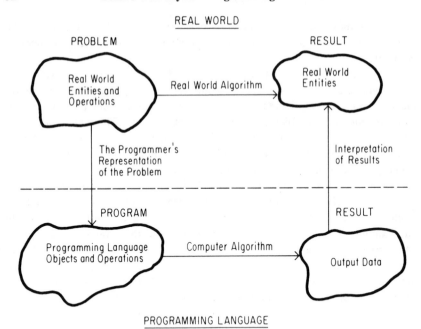

Fig. 2.4   Model for a typical programming task

To avoid surprises for the reader, a programmer must be conscious that part of his job is to map real world entities (for example, prices, temperatures, dollars, dates, and people's names) into the constructs of the BASIC language (for example, numbers and strings). A programmer must not only choose a particular representation for an entity but must make sure that an operation validly represented in BASIC has meaning when applied to the original entity. For example, you can perform all arithmetic operations on numeric data. But while you can subtract two dollar amounts to get another dollar amount, it does not make sense to multiply two dollar amounts or to take the square root of a dollar amount.

More generally (see Fig. 2.4), the input to any program represents some class of real world entities: chess squares, wages, row numbers, cards, colors, and the like. A computation is required to transform these entities into other entities; for example, a chess move, an amount of money, a new row number, a card played, another color, and the like. The computer, however, can operate only in limited ways and on a limited set of entities like strings or integers. Thus, it is necessary to transform the real world set of entities and operations into a program containing computer entities and operations. We shall say that a program is "straightforward" or "natural" or "not tricky" if each step in the computer algorithm has a simple correspondence to a step in a real world algorithm that a person would use to solve the problem.

Straightforwardness and naturalness are closely connected to the clarity and readability of programs. The programmer soon learns that one of the hardest chores of programming is understanding another programmer's code. Often programs do not accurately reflect the real world algorithm corresponding to the numerical, array, logical, or string operations that are required for their computer implementation.

Try looking at any program that you wrote a month ago without peeking at the comments or the documentation. See if you immediately understand all of its details. Now imagine what it would be like for someone else who hadn't seen the program before. Clarity is a godsend to anyone who has to document, debug, extend, use, grade, or otherwise handle a computer program. Unless a program printout is being used by only one person, clarity is a double godsend to anyone having to use the program other than the original programmer.

For example, consider the following problem. Given a deck of 51 cards, we are asked to find the rank of the missing card (by computer, of course!). The deck is stored in a 51-element array called D (Deck). To make things simple, two functions, FNV (returns a value) and FNN (returns a name), are assumed to be defined. FNV takes the desired rank name of a card as its argument and maps the rank of the card into a numeric value: 1 (for ace), 2 (for deuce), . . . , 13 (for king). FNN does the reverse operation. Example 2.12 depicts two pieces of code, both of which claim to do the job correctly. Your problem is to discover *why* each one gives the correct result.

Example 2.12 Two Card-Counting Algorithms to Find the Rank of a Missing Card

```
            EXAMPLE 2.12A   TRICKY CARD COUNT

100 REM
110 REM     **   LOCAL VARIABLES -
120 REM     **   C1 - COUNTER OF RANKS
130 REM     **   R1 - RANK
140 REM     **   N1 - NUMBER OF CARDS
150 REM     **   N2 - NUMBER OF RANKS
160 REM     **   D  - DECK OF CARDS
170 REM     **   X  - MISSING CARD
180 REM
190 REM     **   FUNCTIONS -
200 REM     **   FNV - RETURNS THE RANK VALUE OF A CARD
210 REM     **   FNN - RETURNS THE RANK NAME OF A CARD
220 REM
230         DIM D(51)
240         DATA 51, 13
250 REM
260             READ N1, N2
270 REM
280             LET C1 = 0
290 REM
300             FOR I = 1 TO N1
310                 LET R1 = FNV(D$(I))
320                 LET C1 = C1 + R1
330                 IF (C1 < N2) GOTO 350
340                     LET C1 = C1 - N2
350             NEXT I
360 REM
370             LET X$ = FNN$(N2 - C1)
380             PRINT 'A(N) ', X$, ' IS MISSING'
390 REM
400 REM
410         END
```

Example 2.12 Two Card-Counting Algorithms (Cont'd.)

```
                    EXAMPLE 2.12B   NATURAL CARD COUNT

      100 REM
      110 REM    **   LOCAL VARIABLES -
      120 REM    **   C1 - COUNTER OF RANKS
      130 REM    **   R1 - RANK
      140 REM    **   N1 - NUMBER OF CARDS
      150 REM    **   N2 - NUMBER OF RANKS
      160 REM    **   N3 - NUMBER OF SUITS
      170 REM    **   D  - DECK OF CARDS
      180 REM    **   X  - MISSING CARD
      190 REM
      200 REM    **   FUNCTIONS -
      210 REM    **   FNV - RETURNS THE RANK VALUE OF A CARD
      220 REM    **   FNN - RETURNS THE RANK NAME OF A CARD
      230 REM
      240           DIM D(51), C1(13)
      250           DATA 51, 13, 4
      260 REM
      270             READ N1, N2, N3
      280 REM
      290             FOR R1 = 1 TO N2
      300                 LET C1(R1) = 0
      310             NEXT R1
      320 REM
      330             FOR I = 1 TO N1
      340                 LET R1 = FNV(D$(I))
      350                 LET C1(R1) = C1(R1) + 1
      360             NEXT I
      370 REM
      380            TO N1
      390                 IF (C1(R1)>= N3) GOTO 410
      400                     LET X$ = FNN$(R1)
      410             NEXT R1
      420 REM
      430             PRINT 'A(N) ', X$, ' IS MISSING'
      440 REM
      450 REM
      460          END
```

Example 2.12b is obviously correct. In the real world, it corresponds to keeping a checklist of each rank and checking off the card ranks, one by one, until the deck is exhausted. Then the checklist is scanned to find out which card has been checked fewer than four times, and the selected rank is printed.

Example 2.12a is also correct but far less straightforward. It has almost no correspondence to typical card table operations. It runs through the deck keeping a modulo 13 count of all the ranks and afterwards subtracting this count from 13 to get the rank of the missing card. If you are not convinced, try it.

Another area where natural programs have an advantage is that of *extendability*. Because a natural algorithm is analogous to real world operations, extensions using these operations can often be made easily. Since a tricky algorithm usually depends on specific properties of numbers or strings, it usually cannot be applied to cases other than the original problem.

Example 2.12 illustrates this point well. Say that we now wish to extend the given programs to find the ranks of N missing cards from a deck containing fewer than 51 cards. The algorithm of Example 2.12b can be extended quite

Example 2.13 Extension of the Natural Card Count

```
100 REM
110 REM    **   LOCAL VARIABLES -
120 REM    **   C1 - COUNTER
130 REM    **   R1 - RANK
140 REM    **   N1 - NUMBER OF CARDS
150 REM    **   N2 - NUMBER OF RANKS
160 REM    **   N3 - NUMBER OF SUITS
170 REM    **   D  - DECK OF CARDS
180 REM    **   X  - MISSING CARD
190 REM
200 REM    **   FUNCTIONS -
210 REM    **   FNV - RETURNS THE RANK VALUE OF A CARD
220 REM    **   FNN - RETURNS THE RANK NAME OF A CARD
230 REM
240            DIM D(51), C1(13)
250            DATA 13, 4
260 REM
270                READ N2, N3
280                INPUT N1
290 REM
300                FOR R1 = 1 TO N2
310                    LET C1(R1) = 0
320                NEXT R1
330 REM
340                FOR I = 1 TO N1
350                    LET R1 = FNV(D$(I))
360                    LET C1(R1) = C1(R1) + 1
370                NEXT I
380 REM
390                FOR R1 = 1 TO N1
400                    IF (C1(R1) >= N3)  GOTO 450
410                        LET X$ = FNN$(R1)
420                        PRINT 'A(N) ', X$, ' IS MISSING'
430                        LET C1(R1) = C1(R1) + 1
440                        GOTO 400
450                NEXT R1
460 REM
470 REM
480 .          END
```

readily, as shown in Example 2.13. In the corresponding real world, the sweep of the checklist is the same as before except that when we find that a card is missing, we print it, show that we have covered it by adding it back into the checklist, and see if any others of that rank are missing.

Example 2.12a *cannot* be extended, even to cover the case of two missing cards. The validity of the algorithm is based on the condition that there is only one missing card. With only one missing card, the difference between 13 and the count must be the rank of the missing card. With two or more missing cards, the sum of the ranks of the missing cards may be split in an arbitrary number of ways. In short, this algorithm fails because it is based on the particular properties of numbers instead of the properties of cards.

Before concluding the discussion of this proverb, remember that when tricks are indiscriminately employed, good structure, flexibility, and clarity are frequently lost. Merging two or more modules of code in order to wring out those "extra lines" or adding a few lines in order to gain efficiency are both easy ways to prevent anyone from following the program. Not mentioning the extra time needed to develop the special wrinkle and the extra testing time needed to check the new and often subtle boundary confitions, are you sure that fewer machine instructions or faster machine execution are likely?

One last point about tricky or clever programming must be mentioned. There are cases where tricky methods are in fact justified, for example, to provide demanded efficiency of execution or economy of storage. However, before you resort to tricky programming, you should have a clear reason for doing so. Moreover, you should estimate the actual gain such programming will yield. Otherwise, you should stick to operations and objects that have a natural analog in the real world.

Proverb 14   PRODUCE GOOD OUTPUT

Any experienced programmer engaged in writing programs for use by others knows that, once his program is working correctly, good output is a must. Few people really care how much time and trouble a programmer has spent in designing and debugging a program. Most people see only the results. Often, by the time a programmer has finished tackling a difficult problem, any output may look great. The programmer knows what it means and how to interpret it. However, the same cannot be said for others, or even for the programmer six months hence.

The point is obvious. After all that work and effort spent in writing a program, don't let it look slipshod by having messy, poorly spaced, or skimpy output. Consider Example 2.14a. The output of this simple program could be incomprehensible without an exact knowledge of the problem definition or the program itself. The output of the program of Example 2.14b, on the other hand, can be clearly understood by anyone.

The moral is simple. Annotate your output so that its meaning can stand on its own.

Example 2.14 Use of Informative Output

```
          EXAMPLE 2.14A   POOR

    100 REM
    110 REM   **   LOCAL VARIABLES
    120 REM   **   S1  - SALESMAN
    130 REM   **   S2  - SALES PER PAY PERIOD
    140 REM   **   A   - AVERAGE NUMBER OF SALES PER WEEK
    150 REM   **   N   - NUMBER OF WEEKS IN PAY PERIOD
    160 REM   **   FNS - FUNCTION TO COMPUTE TOTAL NUMBER OF SALES
    170 REM
    180        DIM S2(4)
    190        DATA 4
    200 REM
    210           READ N
    220 REM
    230           INPUT S1
    240           MAT INPUT S2
    250 REM
```

Example 2.14 Use of Informative Output (Cont'd.)

```
260          LET A = FNS (S2, N)
270          LET A = A / N
280 REM
290          PRINT S1; A
300          MAT PRINT S2
310 REM
320 REM
330       END
340 REM
350 REM
360 REM
370       DEF FNS (V, N)
380 REM
390       DIM V(N)
400 REM
410          LET FNS = 0
420 REM
430          FOR I = 1 TO N
440             LET FNS = FNS + V(I)
450          NEXT I
460 REM
470 REM
480       FNEND


DATA

2704
1030   980 1000   990


OUTPUT

2704 1000
1030   980 1000   990


          EXAMPLE 2.14B   BETTER


100 REM
110 REM    **   LOCAL VARIABLES -
120 REM    **   S1  - SALESMAN
130 REM    **   S2  - SALES PER PAY PERIOD
140 REM    **   A   - AVERAGE NUMBER OF SALES PER WEEK
150 REM    **   N   - NUMBER OF WEEKS IN PAY PERIOD
160 REM    **   FNS - FUNCTION TO COMPUTE TOTAL NUMBER OF SALES
170 REM
180       DIM S2(4)
190       DATA 4
200 REM
210          READ N
220          INPUT S1
230          MAT INPUT S2
240          PRINT '   SALESMAN #'; S1; ' SOLD -'
250          FOR I = 1 TO N
260             PRINT '      $ '; S2(I); ' IN WEEK'; I
270          NEXT I
280 REM
290          LET A = FNS (S2, N)
300          LET A = A / N
310 REM
320          PRINT
330          PRINT '   AVERAGE WEEKLY SALES   $ '; A
```

Example 2.14 Use of Informative Output (Cont'd.)

```
340 REM
350 REM
360        END
370 REM
380 REM
390 REM
400        DEF FNS (V, N)
410 REM
420        DIM V(N)
430 REM
440           LET FNS = 0
450 REM
460           FOR I = 1 TO N
470              LET FNS = FNS + V(I)
480           NEXT I
490 REM
500 REM
510        FNEND


DATA

2704
1030   980 1000   990


OUTPUT

    SALESMAN #   2704     SOLD -
          $ 1030 IN WEEK  1
          $  980 IN WEEK  2
          $ 1000 IN WEEK  3
          $  990 IN WEEK  4

    AVERAGE WEEKLY SALES  $    1000
```

Proverb 15   HAND-CHECK THE PROGRAM

It can be difficult to convince a programmer that a program should be hand-checked before being run. Yet run-time errors are the hardest to detect, and unless the system provides excellent debugging facilities, using the computer to help is full of hazards. Even in a time-sharing environment, the programmer is well-advised to check out every program completely by hand before running it. He or she may well be surprised at discovering errors like incorrect signs, infinite loops, and unusual conditions leading to program crashes.

The technique is simple. Choose a sample input, then calculate the output as if you were the computer, assuming nothing and using *exactly* what is written. See that each logical unit performs correctly and that the control sequence through the units is correct. If the program is too long or complex to check in its entirety, then check each major section first, and later check the smaller units, assuming that the major sections are correct. When choosing sample input, take special care to include the boundary conditions and other unusual cases. Failure to account for them is one of the most common programming errors.

For example, suppose you were asked to write a program that takes two nonnegative integers as input—a dividend and a divisor—and prints out two numbers—the integer part of the quotient and the integer remainder.

Assume that BASIC does not have an integer division operator which gives the integer part of a floating point number. That is, given the integer variables D1 (Dividend), D2 (Divisor), Q (Quotient), and R (Remainder), assume that you cannot just say

$$\text{LET } Q = D1/D2$$
$$\text{LET } R = D1 - (Q + D2)$$

As a first pass, consider the program segment in Example 2.15a. Does this work? Obviously it doesn't, for if it did, it wouldn't be in a proverb called "Hand-Check the Program." Checking by hand, we find that the program bombs out in the IF statement. R is initially undefined. (Remember, never assume that the computer assumes anything.) We thus change the program as shown in Example 2.15b.

Does the program work now? Obviously not, or we wouldn't have asked. Checking the boundary conditions by hand, we find that when the divisor is zero,

Example 2.15 Hand-Checking a Program

EXAMPLE 2.15A FIRST ATTEMPT

```
100 REM
110 REM      **   LOCAL VARIABLES -
120 REM      **   D1 - DIVIDEND
130 REM      **   D2 - DIVISOR
140 REM      **   Q  - QUOTIENT
150 REM      **   R  - REMAINDER
160 REM
170              INPUT D1, D2
180 REM
190              LET Q = 0
200 REM
210              IF (R <= D2)  GOTO 260
220                  LET R = R - D2
230                  LET Q = Q + 1
240                  GOTO 210
250 REM
260              PRINT Q, R
270 REM
280 REM
290          END
```

EXAMPLE 2.15B SECOND ATTEMPT

```
100              INPUT D1, D2
110 REM
120              LET R = D1
130              LET Q = 0
140 REM
150              IF (R <= D2)  GOTO 200
160                  LET R = R - D2
170                  LET Q = Q + 1
180                  GOTO 150
190 REM
200              PRINT Q, R
210 REM
220 REM
230          END
```

Example 2.15 Hand-Checking a Program (Cont'd)

```
              EXAMPLE 2.15C   THIRD ATTEMPT


  100 REM
  110 REM    **   LOCAL VARIABLES -
  120 REM    **   D1 - DIVIDEND
  130 REM    **   D2 - DIVISOR
  140 REM    **   Q  - QUOTIENT
  150 REM    **   R  - REMAINDER
  160 REM
  170            INPUT D1, D2
  180 REM
  190            IF (D2 <> 0)  GOTO 230
  200                PRINT 'ATTEMPT TO DIVIDE BY 0***'
  210                GOTO 340
  220 REM
  230            LET R = D2
  240            LET Q = 0
  250 REM
  260            IF (R <= D2)  GOTO 310
  270                LET R = R - D2
  280                LET Q = Q + 1
  290                GOTO 260
  300 REM
  310            PRINT Q, R
  320 REM
  330 REM
  340            END




              EXAMPLE 2.15D   FOURTH ATTEMPT


  100            INPUT D1, D2
  110 REM
  120            IF (D2 <> 0)  GOTO 160
  130                PRINT 'ATTEMPT TO DIVIDE BY 0***'
  140                GOTO 270
  150 REM
  160            LET R = D1
  170            LET Q = 0
  180 REM
  190            IF (R < D2)  GOTO 240
  200                LET R = R - D2
  210                LET Q = Q + 1
  220                GOTO 190
  230 REM
  240            PRINT Q, R
  250 REM
  260 REM
  270            END
```

---

the algorithm doesn't terminate. Since division by zero is undefined, we should process this case separately. It wouldn't be wise to leave the program in an infinite loop, computer time costing what it does. We thus change the program as shown in Example 2.15c.

It still doesn't work. Checking another boundary condition, we find that if the divisor exactly divides the dividend, we always get a quotient of 1 less than the correct value. For example, 10 divided by 5 is 2 with a remainder of 0, not 1 with a remainder of 5. Correcting this error is easy, as shown in Example 2.15d.

This version works. Although the first error probably would have been picked up easily at run time, the other two probably would not have been. Their effects are input-dependent. Can you imagine searching for a data-dependent error in a long program that goes bad only once in a while?

Simply stated, check your program, especially the boundary conditions, before running it.

Proverb 16   PREPARE TO PROVE THE PUDDING

We have advocated the top-down approach to program development. In turn, we now advocate the top-down approach to checking program correctness, which consists of verifying the main program and the upper levels first and the most primitive modules last.

Verifying from the top down should seem obvious, especially if a program is being written top-down. Programs of this type are usually well modularized, and it is unwise to verify lower levels if the upper levels may be incorrect. Since the sections of the program are integral units that can stand on their own, the most important ones should be verified first. A schematic illustration of a program is presented in Fig. 2.5. Encircled sections indicate that the set of enclosed modules is to be considered as a unit. The program has five main modules, each of which can be verified separately. Some of these modules call submodules, which in turn call other more deeply nested modules. The verification process starts with the main program. As upper modules are verified, the process continues through levels until the entire program has been verified. Verifying the entire program in one lump is to be avoided.

What are some of the available BASIC verification aids? Foremost, try to write programs that run correctly the first time, and stick to good programming principles. The better the quality of the initial program, the less likely a serious error will occur, and the more likely you will be able to find those errors that do occur.

Second, there is one verification aid in standard BASIC and on all systems. In computer lingo it is sometimes known as a "selective dump"; technically, it is known as the PRINT statement. These statements can provide snapshots of the program at any point.

Consider Example 2.16, a program for summing the first N positive integers for differing values of N. Clearly, the answers generated by the program are incorrect. The programmer decides to check the main program loop and adds the verification lines shown, which print out the inner loop control variable and the current value of the sum. When the revised program is run, we can easily see that on iteration 1 for the second value of N, the sum is already 22; that is, S (Sum) is not properly initialized. Moving the S initialization statement to just before the inner FOR loop solves the problem.

One popular verification aid available in several implementations is the "trace." Basically, a trace is a facility which will monitor the behavior of prespecified variables or functions. The trace of a variable can monitor any use or

THE PROGRAM P

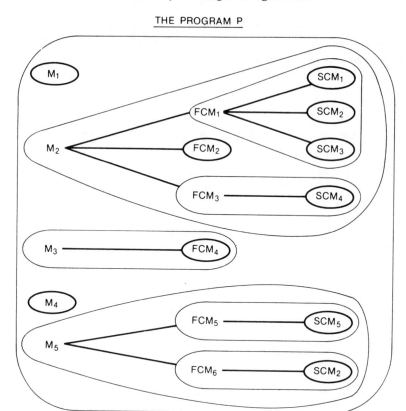

P - The Entire Program   FCM - First Called Submodules
M - Main Modules   SCM - Second Called Submodules

Fig. 2.5   Picture of a program designed top down

change of its value. The trace of a function can monitor each call, its arguments, and its returned value. The programmer can use a trace to verify that functions are being called with proper arguments and correct returned values. In function-oriented programs or programs with recursion, traces can be invaluable. One word of caution: Overuse of the trace feature has been known to produce voluminous output with no useful information.

Systems that implement BASIC usually offer other verification facilities. Does your system support any program design, development, or documentation aids? Does your system support a cross-reference lister, program librarian, test data generator, test supervisor, module testing, execution monitor, or output analyzer package? Be sure to find out what features your system provides, and incorporate them into programs you write. Although it may not be wise to use implementation-dependent features as part of a final program, it would be foolish not to utilize them for verification.

In summary, you can and should make good use of the verification

Example 2.16 Use of Write Statement for Verification

```
PROGRAM

100 REM
110 REM    **   PROGRAM TO SUM THE FIRST N POSITIVE INTEGERS
120 REM    **   FOR M INPUT VALUES OF N (N  = 100)
130 REM
140            LET S = 0
150            INPUT M
160 REM
170            FOR I = 1 TO M
180               INPUT N
190               FOR J = 1 TO N
200                  LET S = S + J
210               NEXT J
220               PRINT 'SUM OF FIRST '; N; ' INTEGERS IS'; S
230            NEXT I
240 REM
250 REM
260        END


OUTPUT

SUM OF FIRST   6 INTEGERS IS    21
SUM OF FIRST   3 INTEGERS IS    27


VERIFICATION LINE INSERTED BEFORE LINE 210

            PRINT ' ITERATION '; J; '    SUM '; S


OUTPUT WITH VERIFICATION

ITERATION    1    SUM    1
ITERATION    2    SUM    3
ITERATION    3    SUM    6
ITERATION    4    SUM   10
ITERATION    5    SUM   15
ITERATION    6    SUM   21
SUM OF FIRST    6 INTEGERS IS    21
ITERATION    1    SUM   22
ITERATION    2    SUM   24
ITERATION    3    SUM   27
SUM OF FIRST    3 INTEGERS IS    27
```

---

facilities in your computer system. Remember, blessed is he who expects the worst, for he shall not be disappointed.

Proverb 17   HAVE SOMEONE ELSE READ THE WORK

This proverb is so important that we considered putting it at the head of the list. Every programmer should realize that programming is by no means a purely personal art. While poor definitions, documentation, and programs can be easy to overlook, they will be quite evident to someone else. Even good programmers stand to gain by having others read the work being produced.

**Example 2.17 The Interpreter Catches One Error, But Who
Catches the Others?**

```
100 REM
110 REM    **   PROGRAM TO FIND THE REAL ROOTS OF THE
120 REM    **   EQUATION (A * (X**2.0)) + (B * X) + C  =  0
130 REM
140            INPUT A, B, C
150            PRINT 'A = '; A, ' B = '; B, ' C = '; C
160 REM
170        IF (A <> 0)   GOTO 270
180            IF (B <> 0)   GOTO 220
190                PRINT 'THIS IS THE DEGENERATE CASE'
200                GOTO 270
210 REM
220                LET X = -C / B
230                PRINT 'ONE REAL ROOT...X = '; X
240                GOTO 270
250 REM
260 REM
270        LET D = (B * B) - (4.0 * A * C)
280 REM
290        IF (D >= 0)   GOTO 330
300            PRINT 'NO REAL ROOTS'
310            GOTO 460
320 REM
330        IF (D > 0)   GOTO 400
340            LET X1 = -B / 2.0 * A
350            LET X2 = X1
360            PRINT 'REAL ROOTS ARE...X1 = ; X1
370            PRINT '                 X2 = ; X2
380            GOTO 460
390 REM
400            LET X1 = (-B + D**.5) / 2.0 * A
410            LET X2 = (-B - D**.5) / 2.0 * A
420            PRINT 'REAL ROOTS ARE...X1 = ; X1
430            PRINT '                 X2 = ; X2
440 REM
450 REM
460        END
```

Having someone else read the work does *not* mean just having someone else read the final code. Even a developing problem definition ought to be read by someone else. The program specifications, the levels of the top-down design, and the test plans you are writing should also be read. All of these projects should be doublechecked by someone else.

The primary benefit of this second reading is that it helps weed out quickly all unwarranted assumptions, unintentional omissions, unnecessary complexities, or just plain mistakes. However, there are other benefits. Both you and your reader can learn good problem-solving and programming techniques from one another. Programming teams that make a point of work-reading foster cooperative communication, maintain team standards more easily, promote quality documentation, and consistently keep abreast of the total work effort.

Consider Example 2.17, which contains two simple but easily made errors. The programmer who wrote the code would find the errors almost impossible to detect by rereading the code yet another time. Try to find them yourself. We contend that work-reading will help prevent such errors from ever disturbing your sleep.

We have a few suggestions for making work-reading more effective. First, remember the proverbs, and point out any violations you see. Second, choose a sample input; then calculate the output as if you were the computer. Assume nothing and use exactly what is written. See that each module performs correctly. If the program is too long or complex to check in its entirety, then check each major section first, and later check the smaller units, assuming that the major sections are correct. Third, take special care to watch for the boundary conditions and other special cases. Failure to account for these is one of the most critical programming errors.

The time and extra care required for work-reading seem a small price to pay for all the benefits listed above. However, at first the practice may seem time-consuming, annoying, and possibly even embarrassing. You must make an extra effort to stick by this proverb for quite a while. Given time, it will come to have an enormous beneficial impact on your work. As a helpful hint we recommend that you practice as a reader for others. Remember, *all aspects of good programming practice are fostered by work-reading.*

Proverb 18 READ THE MANUALS AGAIN

Now why would anyone want to go back and read those boring language or system manuals again? A wise programmer will occasionally do exactly that. After programming for a while, one tends to restrict oneself to a convenient subset of a language or the host computer system. As a result, many useful features may be neglected. Periodically rereading the manuals will help to keep useful features in mind when the need for them arises.

Do you know how BASIC deals with noninteger subscripts? Do you know all the predefined mathematical functions and the file manipulation capabilities? What happens on an array reference bounds error or an ON-GOTO bounds error? What special options are available on your system?

How about the number of significant figures kept by your particular machine? How are overflow and underflow defined and handled; do they cause termination of execution? What is the accuracy of evaluation of numeric expressions? How many characters can be stored within a single string variable? When does your system truncate numeric values? When does it round?

How are user functions defined? Does the interpreter allow more than one parameter? Are multiline functions permitted? Can functions be invoked recursively? If so, how are the recursive calls handled?

Can subroutines be defined to allow passing of parameters? Can subroutines be called recursively?

How much flexibility is permitted in input/output operations? For instance, how does your system handle an attempt to read a character string into a numeric variable? How are the print zones defined? Is formatting allowed on either input or output?

You must, of course, be careful when using unfamiliar or little used features. Be sure you are using them correctly. Do not go overboard for the results may no longer be simple and direct. Nevertheless, we strongly recommend an occasional look at your manuals. You may be pleased with what you find.

Proverb 19   DON'T BE AFRAID TO START OVER

This is the last proverb, but it is of great importance. We dare not dwell on it too long because we hope you will never have to use it.

Sometimes during program development, testing, or modification, it may occur to a programmer that the program he is working with is becoming unusually cumbersome. So many user-requirement changes may have occurred that the problem is now different from what it was originally. Very few, if any, of the programming proverbs may have been applied in developing the program; or perhaps the program produces error after error.

Pruning and restoring a blighted tree is almost an impossible task. The same is true of blighted computer programs. Restoring a structure that has been distorted by patches and deletions or fixing a program with a seriously weak algorithm just isn't worth the time. The best that can result is a long, inefficient, unintelligible program that defies further maintenance. The worst that could result we dare not think of. When you seem hopelessly in trouble, start over. Lessons painfully learned on the old program can be applied to the new one to yield the desired result in far less time with far less trouble.

This last proverb may seem heartless, but don't let your ego stand in the way. Don't be afraid to start over. We mean *really* start over. Don't fall into the trap of trying to convert a bad program into a good one.

EXERCISES

Exercise 2.1   (Define the Problem Completely)
Consider the following program specification:

"Write a program that computes the weight in kilograms of a weight expressed in pounds and ounces."

Upon careful thought, the above specification reveals many points that would be unclear to a programmer. Rewrite the above specification so that *any* two programs written to solve the problem would have *exactly* the same input–output characteristics, for example, the same input format, the same number of significant digits, the same headings, and so forth. (Note: You are to write a program specification, *not* a program; a good definition may require a full page.)

Exercise 2.2   (Define the Problem Completely)

Each of the following program specifications is either missing one or more critical definitions or is unclear, misleading, or confusing. (a) How are the program specifications deficient? (b) Rewrite all or part of one program specification to make it as clear and explicit as possible, that is, so that there can be no doubt as to what the program should do. (c) In general, what does *any* program specification require to make it as clear and explicit as possible?

Program specification 1: Given the following rates of payment, write a program that will compute the monthly commission for a car salesman.

Grade of Salesman	Commission Rate
1	$5.00 + 0.50% for first ten sales $7.50 + 0.75% every subsequent sale
2	$7.50 + 0.75% for first ten sales $10.00 + 1.00% every subsequent sale
3	$10.00 + 1.00% for first ten sales $12.50 + 1.25% every subsequent sale
4	$12.50 + 1.25% for first ten sales $15.00 + 1.50% every subsequent sale
5	$15.00 + 1.50% for first ten sales $17.50 + 1.75% every subsequent sale

The input should be the grade of the salesman and the number of sales he has made for the month. The output should read "THE SALES-MAN'S COMMISSION IS $c," where c is the salesman's commission.

Program specification 2: The Programmer's Equity Life Insurance Company offers policies of $25,000, $50,000, and $100,000. The cost of a policyholder's annual premium is determined as follows. There is a basic fee that depends upon the amount of coverage carried. This is $25 for a $25,000 policy, $50 for a $50,000 policy, and $100 for a $100,000 policy.

In addition to the basic fee, there are two additional charges depending on the age and lifestyle of the policyholder. The first additional charge is determined by multiplying by 2 the policyholder's age minus 21 and then multiplying this by either 1½, 2, or 3 if the policy is at the $25,000, $50,000, or $100,000 level, respectively. The second additional charge is determined by the policyholder's lifestyle, which is a rating of the danger of harm resulting from his occupation and hobbies. This rating is determined by company experts from a questionnaire returned by the policy applicant. They return a rating of from 1 to 5 in steps of 1, with 1 being the safest rating. The charge is then determined by multiplying this rating by 5 and then further multiplying by 1½, 2, or 3 if the policy is either at the $25,000, $50,000, or $100,000 level, respectively. The total premium is found by adding together these separately determined charges.

Write a program to output tables of yearly premium costs for men of ages from 21 to 75 for all amounts of policy value and safety ratings.

Exercise 2.3   (Define the Problem Completely)
Upon careful reading, the problem definition of Example 2.1b shows several deficiencies. The *exact* input–output characteristics are not really fully specified. Describe these deficiencies.

Exercise 2.4   (Use Functions and Subroutines)
Consider a program with the following specification:

> *Input:*   a positive integer N
> *Output:*   the values ΣN, $\Sigma(\Sigma N)$, $\Sigma(\Sigma(\Sigma N))$, and $\Sigma(\Sigma(\Sigma(\Sigma N)))$

where ΣN denotes the sum of the first N integers.

1. Write the program *without* the use of functions or subroutines.
2. Write the program using functions or subroutines. The differences can be quite striking.

Exercise 2.5   (Watch Out for GOTOs)
Restructure the following statement sequence to eliminate most GOTOs and statement numbers and to make the sequence as *short* and clear as possible. (Note: It can be done with only two assignment statements.)

```
100          GOTO 170
110          IF (X <> 0)   GOTO 130
120             GOTO 190
130          IF (X <= M)   GOTO 220
140             GOTO 190
150          PRINT X
160          STOP
170          INPUT X
180          GOTO 110
190          LET X = X**.5
200          LET X = X*X + X
210          GOTO 150
220          LET X = X*X
230          GOTO 200
```

Exercise 2.6   (Watch Out for GOTOs)
Consider the conventional 8 by 8 array representation of a chessboard whose squares are denoted by (1,1), (1,2), . . . , (8,8) and the problem of placing eight queens on the board so that *no* queen can capture *any other*

queen. In chess, a queen can capture another piece if the queen lies on the same row, column, or diagonal as the other piece.

1. Write a program to read in the coordinates of eight queens and print "TRUE" if no queen can capture any other and "FALSE" otherwise.
2. Draw a flow diagram for the program.
3. Score the program according to the following rule:

$$\text{SCORE} = 100 - 10*(\text{number-of-crossing-lines})$$

Exercise 2.7   (Get the Syntax Correct Now)

It is important that a programmer be able to detect simple syntactic errors. Consider the following program to compute PI using the series,

$$\text{PI}^4/96 = 1/1^4 + 1/3^4 + 1/5^4 + \ldots.$$

How many syntactic errors are there? Correct the program so that there are no errors.

```
100           LET N = 0
110           IF (T >= E)  GOTO 170
120             LAT N = N + 1
130             LET T = 1 / (2N - 1)**X
140             S = S + T
150             GOTO 110
160 REM
170             LET P = FNS(FNS(D*S))
180       END
```

Exercise 2.8   (Get the Syntax Correct Now)

Which of the following examples are syntactically correct instances of the given BASIC categories? Correct the erroneous examples. If possible, you should assume *any* suitable specification statements needed to make a construct correct.

```
(1)    ARITHMETIC EXPRESSION
          F(F)

(2)    ARITHMETIC EXPRESSION
          P(Q) + X**Y**Z - 1/2

(3)    IF STATEMENT
          IF ((X AND Y) > 4)  GOTO 100

(4)    STATEMENT FUNCTION
          FNF (A,X) = A(X) * A(X+1) * A(X+2)

(5)    STATEMENT FUNCTION
          FNF (G, E, FNF) = G + G*E + G*E*FNF

(6)    MULTI-LINE FUNCTION
          DEF FNF(X,A)
              LET A = A / 5
              LET X = A**2
          FNEND

(7)    DATA STATEMENT
          DATA X / 1 /
```

```
(8)    ASSIGNMENT STATEMENT
          LET X = 'STRING VARIABLE'

(9)    ASSIGNMENT STATEMENT
          LET X$ = 10

(10)   GOTO'S
       100 GOTO 200
       150 LET X = 3
       175 PRINT X
       200 GOTO 150
```

Exercise 2.9   (Plan for Change)

Consider a program to compute the gravitational force F exerted between two planets M_1 and M_2 located (over time) at different orbital distances from each other. In particular, let

$$M_1 = \text{mass of planet } 1 = 6 \times 10^{24}$$
$$M_2 = \text{mass of planet } 2 = 8 \times 10^{25}$$
$$G = \text{gravitational constant} = 6.7 \times 10^{-11}$$
$$F = G * M_1 * M_2 / (R \uparrow 2)$$

Write a program to output F for values of R varying from $100 * 10^8$ to $110 * 10^8$ in increments of $0.01 * 10^8$ such that all constants are specified in a data statement and *no* constant terms are recomputed.

Exercise 2.10   (Produce Good Output)

The following input/output was generated by the use of a working program in a time-sharing environment:

Input:	WHAT IS N1 AND N2?	
	5,10	
Output:	5	25
	6	36
	7	49
	8	64
	9	81
	10	100

Rewrite the input/output so that the average "man on the street" would be able to understand what the input numbers 5 and 10 represent and what the output means.

Exercise 2.11   (Have Someone Else Read the Work)

Describe two more advantages to having someone else read the work you produce during the various phases of a programming project (see Proverb 17). Describe two disadvantages or bottlenecks.

Exercise 2.12   (Read the Manuals Again)

Reread your BASIC manual and find three features that you had forgotten or did not know existed. Give an example of how each would be most useful.

Exercise 2.13   (Read the Manuals Again)

Answer precisely the following questions with reference to your BASIC manual:

1. How many dimensions can an array have?
2. What is a legal subscript?
3. Are matrix commands available?
4. How many significant digits are kept for REAL numbers?
5. Is multiple assignment allowed?

Exercise 2.14   (Several Proverbs)

The following program performs a simple, well-known computation. Rewrite the program so that it clearly illuminates the intended computation. In the process, watch out for GOTOs, and produce good output.

```
100          GOTO 140
110          INPUT A
120          F = A * A
130          GOTO 170
140          INPUT B
150          LET G = B * B
160          GOTO 110
170          IF ((A <= 0) OR (B <= 0))   GOTO 220
180          LET C = F + G
190          LET D = C**.5
200          PRINT D
210 REM
220          STOP
230    END
```

Exercise 2.15   (Several Proverbs)

Write a program that determines whether an input string is a palindrome. A palindrome is a string that reads the same forwards and backwards. For example, LEVEL is a palindrome but PALINDROME is not. When the program is running correctly, score it using the following formula:

$$SCORE = 100 - (5*\text{times-resubmitted})$$
$$- (2*\text{number-of-lines-changed})$$

Exercise 2.16   (Several Proverbs)

Usually, a complex mathematical expression can be coded as a single arithmetic expression. However, for the sake of clarity it is often advantageous to split up a lengthy arithmetic expression and use intermediate variables. Give an example where clarity is gained with the use of intermediate variables. Give an example where the obvious result is program efficiency. Give an example where the use of inappropriate or excessive intermediate variables causes confusion.

Exercise 2.17   (Guess the Proverb)

The following program is supposed to have the following characteristics:

Input: a sequence of nonzero integers terminated by the integer zero
Output: the MEAN

$$(\sum_{i=1}^{n} x_i) / n$$

and standard deviation of the integers in the sequence:

$$SQRT((\sum_{i=1}^{n} x^2) / n - MEAN^2)$$

```
100          LET A = B = C = D
110          LET D = F = G = 0.0
120          INPUT G
130          IF (G = 999) GOTO 190
140             LET A = A + G
150             LET B = B + 1
160             LET C = C + C + G**2
170             IF (G > F)   GOTO 130
180          LET D = A / B
190          LET E = (C / B - A**2)**(1/2)
200          LET I = F - D / F
210          PRINT E, E
220       END
```

Of all the programming proverbs, which *single* proverb, if properly followed, would be most valuable in converting the above program to a good
program? (Note: There really *is* a best answer.)

TOP-DOWN PROGRAMMING

"There is a certain method in this madness."

Horace: *Satires* II.iii

This chapter presents a technique of program development generally known as top-down programming. The top-down approach presented here is based on the notions of "structured programming" of Dijkstra [Ref. D1] and "stepwise refinement" of Wirth [Ref. W2]. While the technique is not a panacea for all programming ills, it does offer strong guidelines for an intelligent approach to a programming problem.

Before coding, every programmer must have in hand a complete statement of the problem, a well-planned documentation system, and a clear design strategy. The input format, legal and illegal fields, output files, reports, program messages, and the mapping from all various input data situations to their correct outputs must be described in detail. Furthermore, the overall algorithm must also be determined before coding. It is senseless to start coding a program without such a complete attack on the problem.

Given a solid problem definition and an overall program design, the top-down approach is a method for developing computer programs in any programming language. In brief, the approach has the following characteristics:

1. *Design in Levels.* The programmer designs the program in *levels,* where a level consists of one or more modules. A module is always "complete," although it may reference unwritten submodules. The first level is a complete "main program." A lower level refines or develops unwritten modules in the upper level. In other words, the modules of a successive level consist of the submodules referenced in the prior level. The programmer may look several levels ahead to determine the best way to design the level at hand.

2. *Initial Language Independence.* The programmer initially uses expressions (often in English) that are relevant to the problem solution, even though the expressions cannot be directly transliterated into code. From statements that are machine and language independent, the programmer moves toward a final machine implementation in a programming language.

3. *Postponment of Details to Lower Levels.* The programmer concentrates on critical broad issues at the initial levels and postpones details (for example, choice of specific algorithms or intermediate data representations) until lower levels.

4. *Formalization of Each Level.* Before proceeding to a lower level, the programmer ensures that the ''program'' in its current stage of development is a ''formal'' statement. In most cases, this means a program that calls unwritten submodules with all arguments spelled out. This step ensures that further sections of the program will be developed independently, without having to change the specifications or the interfaces between modules.

5. *Verification of Each Level.* After generating the modules of a new level, the programmer verifies the developing formal statement of the program. This ensures that errors pertinent to the current level of development will be detected at their own level.

6. *Successive Refinements.* Each level of the program is refined, formalized, and verified successively until the programmer obtains a completed program that can be transformed easily into code.

One should note several things about the top-down approach. First, the entire problem and its overall solution are presumed to be understood (see Proverbs 1 through 4). It is senseless to start programming until there is a complete understanding of the problem and a complete general plan of attack. Such an understanding allows the programmer to write the program without losing sight of the overall goal.

Second, at the upper levels, the approach is machine and language independent, and the programmer is not constrained by the details of a programming language. He or she is writing the upper levels using a notation that meaningfully solves the problem, although it might not be understood by a language processor. The programmer's use of a particular notation involves no sacrifice. At each level the statements produced still represent a complete program in some sense. All that is lacking is the machine capable of executing the statements.

Third, at each level of design, informal notation must be formalized as a hypothetical, but explicitly specified, procedure. Specification involves a complete listing of all input and output arguments.

Fourth, at each level the programmer must verify the program in its present form so that further refinements will be absolutely correct with respect to previously designed levels. This ensures that oversights will be detected in their proper context.

For example, suppose that a programmer is working at an intermediate level and generates the following informal statement:

case day-of-the-week *of*
        Monday: generate last week's data summary
        Tuesday: do nothing
        Wednesday: update usage file
        Thursday: process new data
        Friday: generate lab item reports
        Saturday: generate weekly breakage statistics
        Sunday: do nothing
   end

The language of this statement is far removed from a programming language. On the other hand, the statement is perfectly clear to the programmer in that it reflects a portion of the desired code. The programmer must elaborate on the required inputs and expected outputs for the procedures like ''generate lab item reports'' and ''update usage file.'' The next levels of refinement must develop each procedure.

The process of solving a problem using the top-down approach can be graphically represented by two trees. The first of them, illustrated in Fig. 3.1, represents the overall program development process. The topmost level, P_0, represents the general conception of the problem. The branches at each successive level of the tree represent the alternative design decisions that the programmer can make. The paths down the tree represent all possible correct programs to solve the given problem. The top-down approach allows the programmer to make design decisions starting from the P_0 level and to follow the tree downward with successive refinements to construct a good solution. At each level the programmer examines the alternative branches and chooses the one that

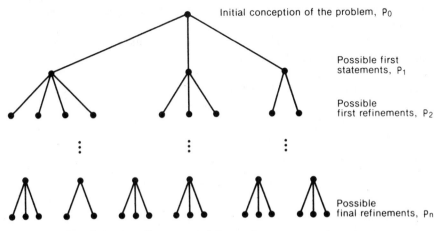

Fig. 3.1   Overall structure of the top-down programming process

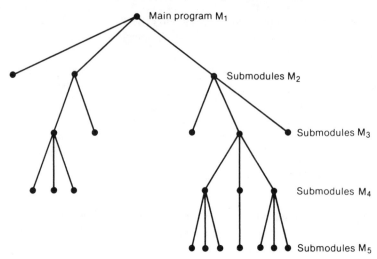

Fig. 3.2   Top-down structure for a specific program

appears most suitable. However, if at any time the choice of any branch seems unwise, it is possible to backtrack up the tree one or more levels and select an alternative solution. The top-down process for a specific problem is thus a sequence of design decisions from P_0 to a specific final program.

The second tree illustrating the top-down approach, shown in Fig. 3.2, represents the hierarchical structure of a specific program for which five levels were needed. The top node is the main program, and the nodes at each successive level are the refined submodules that were introduced but undeveloped in the prior level. By the time the bottom level is reached, we have all the modules that comprise the final program.

There is, of course, a correspondence between the two trees. A single path from P_0 to a particular design choice in P_n in Fig. 3.1 is expanded and described in detail in Fig. 3.2.

The top-down approach is a programming technique that can be widely applied for good results. The technique does not necessarily guarantee the best solution, but it does provide a good structure for solving programming problems. The rest of this chapter will be devoted to an example that illustrates precisely how the top-down method is used to write well-structured modular programs. The example also demonstrates that the method is, by and large, language independent.

KRIEGSPIEL CHECKERS

General Nicklaus C. Roht, President of the state of Atad, has just purchased a Universal 6 computer for his small country. He decides that the first programming job must be performed for the state's national game, Kriegspiel checkers. The General's chairperson of the commission on recreational activities, Charles D. Coleman, is placed in charge of the project. Mr. Coleman puts the state's most experienced program designer, Dr. Irene B. "Top-Down" Malcolm, in charge of the actual programming.

Mr. Coleman, a loyal servant of the state of Atad, prepares a general statement of the problem:

> In Kriegspiel checkers* each player sits in an isolated area, having a separate board containing only his own pieces. Each move must follow the conventional rules for the game of checkers. However, as each player proposes a move, a third person, the referee, tells the player that either (a) the proposed move is legal, and the opponent will be directed to move; (b) the proposed move is illegal, and the player must propose another move; or (c) the proposed move wins and the game is over.

> Using the conventional rules for Kriegspiel checkers, each game is quite long. The state of Atad uses the following additional rules: (a) In addition to winning a game by capturing or blocking all of the opponent's pieces, a player also wins by getting the first king. (b) When a player proposes a legal jump that is part of a multiple jump, the referee informs the player that a further jump is required and the next square must be entered; the player then continues to propose further squares until the multiple jump is completed.

> The program must "know" and enforce the rules of checkers, that is, ensure that black always moves first, insist that a jump be made when one is possible, verify the legality of moves, determine when the game is over, and so forth.

> Furthermore, the program must accept moves in a format familiar to the players. A move consists of two numbers corresponding to squares on a standard checkerboard. The first number denotes the square of the moving piece, and the second number is its destination square. The program must also output "messages" based on whether the proposed move is legal or not, requires a jump continuation, or terminates the game.

> On top of all this, the General insists that the program be operational five weeks from Friday.

As an aid, a picture of a numbered checkerboard has been supplied by Mr. Coleman. This is given in Fig. 3.3.

FUNCTIONAL SPECIFICATION

A professional programmer and a strong advocate of the top-down approach, Irene is calm in the face of General Roht's demands. Despite the fact that a program must be ready in five weeks, she has seen too many programming

---

*For readers who play checkers, the Kriegspiel variant is much more interesting than it at first appears.

BLACK

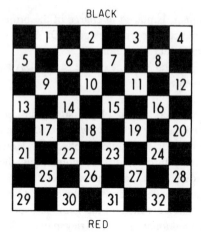

RED

Fig. 3.3   Standard checkerboard numbering system

delays and poor programs caused by a poor problem analysis. Since she is facing a tight schedule, Irene feels all the more strongly that she must revise the given definition and get as complete a functional specification as possible.

Irene realizes that the inputs for the Kriegspiel program are quite simple. Nevertheless she knows that it is all too easy to overlook some critical cases and she therefore decides to examine them in some detail. In simple form, the inputs are a series of pairs of numbers: The first number represents the square designating a player's piece, and the second number represents the square to which that piece is to be moved. Of course, some of the pairs representing a move will result in a move that is illegal on a given board configuration.

Irene quickly notices that the players might input numbers that are too large to correspond with a square on the checkerboard. She decides to keep a list of such possibilities on her ''undesired events list.'' Further, she is aware that users can easily make typographical errors. As such, it is possible that some of the proposed moves may contain characters that are not numbers at all. She adds this possibility to her list.

With these two simple cases in mind, Irene knows that she must think quite carefully about the kinds of errors the users can make in using this program. The human engineering of this program is very important to Irene. What if the user inputs no separator between square numbers? What if the user inputs too many numbers? What if the user accidently hits a carriage return and inputs no square number at all? After some thought, Irene decides to spell out carefully all of the possible input situations. She itemizes these in the form of a table, which is given in Fig. 3.4. Of some note, she decides to allow any trailing string of characters to be given after a proposed move; this allows a player to annotate a game with running comments.

Irene now feels comfortable enough to specify the required outputs for the program. For this program, the outputs are indeed simple, merely messages printed to each player. There are many possible messages, and she believes that it

Input Field	Possible Values	Error Conditions
Normal (2-square) move		
Leading string	Empty	None
First square number	1 ≤ integer ≤ 32	Number too large or too small; contains a non-numeric character
Separator string	A space or comma	Does not contain a space or comma
Second square number	1 ≤ integer ≤ 32	Number too large or too small; contains a non-numeric character
Trailing string	Any string of characters	None
Jump Continuation (1-square) Move		
Leading string	Empty	None
First square number	1 ≤ integer ≤ 32	Number too large or too small; contains a non-numeric character
Trailing string	Any string of characters	None

Fig. 3.4   Format for input lines for Kriegspiel program

is important to determine these messages now. After all, they really should be approved by Mr. Coleman. There are messages indicating that a move must be entered by a player, that a move is legal, that a move is illegal, that a move contains characters that are not understandable by the program, that a square number is out of range, that a move is a jump and requires further inputs, and that the game is won by one of the players.

Irene decides that most messages should be short, for after repetitive use, frequent long messages can be quite annoying to a player. Furthermore, some of the messages should give the user quite specific information, especially in those cases where the user makes an error. She prepares a complete list of output messages for the program and itemizes these messages in the form of a table, given in Fig. 3.5.

Having completed the details of the format and contents of the various inputs and outputs, Irene now describes the mapping of input situations into output responses. Such a description is invaluable to the programmer who develops the ultimate program. Irene's description, given in Fig. 3.6, consists of nested conditions that describe the actions and output response to each input situation.

The functional specification of user requirements is done! Irene happily reviews her results and collects them into a draft for the documentation manual.

Reason for Message	Message
Introductory message for player with black pieces	WELCOME TO KRIEGSPIEL CHECKERS! ENTER YOUR FIRST MOVE XX XX
Introductory message for player with red pieces	WELCOME TO KRIEGSPIEL CHECKERS! YOUR OPPONENT WILL TAKE THE FIRST MOVE
Prompt player for a normal (2-square) move	IT'S YOUR TURN TO MOVE XX XX
Prompt player for a (1-square) jump continuation	YOUR JUMP MUST BE CONTINUED ENTER JUMP SQUARE XX
Acknowledge legal move	YOU HAVE COMPLETED A LEGAL MOVE AND YOUR OPPONENT HAS BEEN ASKED TO MOVE
Nonnumeric characters in input square	***NONNUMERIC CHARACTERS IN SQUARE***
Illegal square number	***SQUARE NUMBER OUT OF RANGE***
No space or comma between square numbers	***NO SPACE OR COMMA BETWEEN SQUARES***
Jump exists and has not been taken	A JUMP IS AVAILABLE AND YOU MUST TAKE IT
Illegal move	TRY AGAIN XX XX
Illegal jump continuation	ILLEGAL JUMP CONTINUATION
Piece captured	PIECE CAPTURED FROM SQUARE:
Losing message	SORRY ... YOUR OPPONENT HAS WON THE GAME!!!
Winning message	CONGRATULATIONS ... YOU HAVE WON THE GAME!!!

Fig. 3.5   Output messages for Kriegspiel program

A copy is sent to Mr. Coleman. Irene drops off other copies to members of the operations board and to one or two of her colleagues for a quick but careful review. Top-down development cannot begin until all criticisms and problems are disposed of.

Just as she is finishing the condition-action table, a new programmer, Dorothy E. Clark, drops in and notices the amount of work Irene is faced with. "Why are you bothering with all this?" she asks. "In college, I was told to try to keep things as short and simple as possible." Irene replies that any evident complexity was not introduced by her but exists in the problem itself. The definition of the problem will not be perfect—what is?—but it will be so close that it is unlikely that programming changes will have to be made later during top-down development or coding. Irene also points out that thinking now will not

Action	Print introductory message to each player, and prompt player for a normal (2-square) move.
Condition 1	Game has not been won and a normal (2-square) move is required.
Action	Prompt player for a normal (2-square) move.
Condition 1.1	First field of input line is not a number.
Action	Print message indicating illegal characters.
Condition 1.2	First field is a number that is not a legal square number.
Action	Print message indicating square number out of range.
Condition 1.3	Separator is not a blank or comma.
Action	Print message indicating illegal separator.
Condition 1.4	Second field is not a number.
Action	Print message indicating illegal characters.
Condition 1.5	Second field is not a legal square number.
Action	Print message indicating illegal square number.
Condition 1.6	Second field is a legal square number.
Condition 1.6.1	Move is illegal on the current board configuration.
Action	Print message indicating illegal move.
Condition 1.6.2	Move is a legal nonjump but a jump exists.
Action	Print message that a jump must be taken.
Condition 1.6.3	Move is a legal nonjump.
Action	Print message indicating a completed legal move, process the move, and prompt the opponent.
Condition 1.6.4	Move is a legal jump and does not require a continuation.
Action	Print message indicating that a piece was captured and that a legal move has been completed, process the move, and prompt the opponent.
Condition 1.6.5	Move is a legal jump and requires a continuation.
Action	Print message indicating that a piece was captured, and process a jump continuation.
Condition 2	Game has not been won and a jump continuation (1-square) move is required.
Action	Prompt player for a jump continuation (1-square) move.
Condition 2.1	The jump square field is not a number.
Action	Print message indicating illegal characters.
Condition 2.2	The jump square field is not a legal square number.
Action	Print message indicating square out of range.
Condition 2.3	The jump continuation square is not legal.

Fig. 3.6   Mapping of input situations to output responses for Kriegspiel checkers program

Action	Print message for illegal jump continuation.
Condition 2.4	The jump continuation square is legal.
Action	Print message acknowledging legal continuation and process move.
Condition 3	Game has been won.
Action	Print winning and losing messages.

Fig. 3.6   Mapping of input situations (Cont'd.)

only save time later but, more important, will help produce a better program. In addition, a careful functional specification will describe the system as seen by the user. Both Mr. Coleman and the operations board have a *complete* description of the external characteristics of the entire program.

Irene is exhausted after writing the functional specification. Since it is almost 4 o'clock anyway, she decides to leave early for a weekend conference dealing with advances in programming languages.

PROGRAM DEVELOPMENT

When Irene returns on Monday, she decides to bring in Dorothy Clark to do the actual top-down development of the Kriegspiel program. Irene meets with Dorothy and explains that the problem is fully specified. Moreover, as a part of normal practice, she tells Dorothy that they will work together closely at the beginning of the top-down development. Irene gives Dorothy a copy of the draft functional specifications and a brief exposition of the top-down approach to programming. She asks Dorothy to give these a careful reading and return the day after next to begin the actual work.

When Dorothy returns, she surprises Irene with the following initial top-down development of the program, P_1:

P_1 *(First pass)*

initialize program variables

10   get a proposed move

if move is not legal
  then goto 10
  else process the move

if the game is not over
  then change players and *goto* 10

end the game and stop

Irene is pleased but notes some problems with the first pass. First, Dorothy's P_1 mentions the initialization of some program variables but does not specify which variables are to be initialized and which messages are to be printed. Second, no mention is made of whether a legal move is in fact a part of a jump situation in which the player must input the squares to continue the jump. In addition, "process the move" is a nebulous subroutine, one that even Dorothy will admit is in need of formalization. Irene and Dorothy work together to produce the following revision:

$$P_1 \ (Formal)$$

gosub INITIALIZE(PLAYER,BOARD)
write (INTRODUCTORY-MESSAGES)

10   input MOVE from PLAYER

if MOVE is not on board
    then goto 10

if NOT LEGAL-MOVE(PLAYER,BOARD,MOVE)
    then write (ILLEGAL-MOVE-MSG)
        goto 10

gosub UPDATE-BOARD(PLAYER,BOARD,MOVE)
if LEGAL-JUMP(PLAYER,BOARD,MOVE) and
    JUMP-CAN-BE-CONTINUED(PLAYER,BOARD,MOVE)
    then gosub CONTINUE-THE-JUMP(PLAYER,BOARD,MOVE)

if NO-KING(BOARD,PLAYER) and MOVES-LEFT(BOARD,
    OPPONENT)
    then swap PLAYERS
        inform (PLAYER) of completed move
        prompt (OPPONENT) for next move
        goto 10

write (WINNING-MSG) for PLAYER,
    (LOSING-MSG) for OPPONENT

stop

Irene is still not pleased with this version of the program. For one thing, the current version calls for one subroutine to check for a legal move and a later subroutine to check if the legal move was a jump and the jump can be continued. At a high level concern for efficiency, it is clear to Irene that the check for a legal move must also include a check for a jump which may need to be continued if it is part of a multiple jump. So why recompute this frequently executed test after the move has already been determined to be legal? She decides that the best course of action is to have a single subroutine to check for the legality of the move and return two flags, one that indicates whether the move was legal and one that indicates whether the move was in fact a jump that must be continued.

Irene also notices a slight error in the current version of P_1. The variable OPPONENT occurs in the code but has never been given a value. Obviously, the OPPONENT is the other PLAYER. This must be spelled out. Further, the BOARD is common to almost every subprogram and really should be global to the entire program.

Irene deliberately postpones decisions about data representations for the board and the players. Such decisions are usually limiting, since there is a tendency to program around the properties of the representation.

With these and other considerations Dorothy and Irene agree on the final version P_1. Cautioned by the unobserved bug in P_1, they carefully check the final version of P_1 to ensure that the "program" at this level is indeed correct.

$$P_1 \ (Final \ Pass)$$

```
        global BOARD
        PLAYER = BLACK
        OPPONENT = RED
        write (INTRODUCTORY-MESSAGES)

10      input MOVE from PLAYER

        if MOVE is not on board
            then goto 10

        gosub CHECK-LEGAL-MOVE
                using (PLAYER,MOVE)
                giving (LEGAL-MOVE-FLAG, CONTINUE-JUMP-FLAG)

        if (LEGAL-MOVE-FLAG is not on)
            then write (ILLEGAL-MOVE-MSG)
                goto 10

        gosub UPDATE-BOARD (PLAYER, MOVE)
        if (CONTINUE-JUMP-FLAG is on)
            then gosub CONTINUE-THE-JUMP (PLAYER, MOVE)

        if NO-KING-FOR(PLAYER) and MOVES-LEFT-FOR(OPPONENT)
            then inform (PLAYER) of completed move
                prompt (OPPONENT) for new move
                swap (PLAYER, OPPONENT)
                goto 10
```

write (WINNING-MSG) for PLAYER
(LOSING-MSG) for OPPONENT

stop

Data Representation

Before Dorothy and Irene can proceed, they must determine the "specific structure of the data representations." This six-dollar phrase means that they must figure out a way to represent the checkerboard and the players' pieces in the program. Remember that players use the standard checkerboard of Fig. 3.3. There is a great temptation to code the standard checkerboard numbering system directly into the program, but Irene points out that this is much more difficult than it appears.

First, look at square 10 of Fig. 3.3. A black piece on that square can make a nonjump move to squares 14 or 15. So the possible moves are (10 + 4) = 14, and (10 + 5) = 15, or simply +4 and +5. But from square 15 the black moves are to squares 18 and 19, or simply +3 and +4. A similar situation exists for red, except that the moves are −3,−4 and −4,−5, since the move direction is reversed. They could sort out which moves use the 3,4 rule and which moves use the 4,5 rule, but another problem remains. Black's first row (squares 1 through 4) uses the +4,+5 rule. But what about square 4? Using the +4,+5 rule, 8 is a legal square, but 9 is not.

Dorothy remembers an article she read in *Scientific American* [Ref. S2] that described an ingenious representation for a checkerboard devised by A. L. Samuels (see Fig. 3.7). In this scheme, regardless of the square, the possible

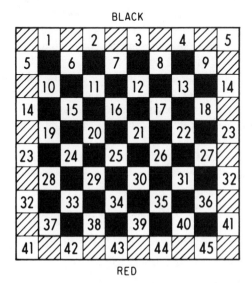

BLACK

RED

Fig. 3.7   Samuel's board numbering for internal representation of a checkerboard

directed moves for black are always +4 and +5, and for red, −4 and −5. The added border squares are "flag" squares. They will contain some value to indicate that they do not represent legal squares. When a proposed move goes from a legal square to a "flag" square, the move can be quickly detected as illegal. The opposite border squares are labeled with the same numbers. This causes no confusion as they are flag squares and need not have distinct numbers.

Although this representation solves many problems, Irene is somewhat troubled. Players use the standard checkerboard in Fig. 3.3, whereas the program must use that of Fig. 3.7. This inconsistency means that input moves will have to be converted to Samuel's representative. Furthermore, the whole situation is somewhat tricky to handle. Irene recalls the proverb, "Think First, Code Later," and decides to give the matter a few days "incubation" time.

Thinking and Problem Solving

Dorothy does some hard thinking.

After some time, she realizes that the board has two distinct uses: as a record of the current status of the game, and as a means for determining legal squares for proposed moves. She notes that, aside from player or opponent pieces on the actual board, the possible legal squares for a player's moves are constant. Constant! Yes! Why not let the possible legal square from each square be stored in a constant array? For example, for a black piece on square 14, the only possible nonjumps are to squares 17 and 18, and the only possible jumps are to squares 21 and 23. As for the current status of the game, she can maintain a separate array to keep track of the current board configuration.

She quickly sketches out this idea in the form of a table, which is given in Fig. 3.8. She notes that some left or right moves have no legal square. This causes no problems, for she can easily have a special value for this case. As for the status of the board, she can represent the conventional (32-square) board layout in the form of a 32-element array.

Irene now has a board representing the current status of the game. But what is she going to put on it? Checkers? Yes, in a sense, but she will have to create a representation for them. She decides to represent the pieces for P1 (player 1) by the number 1, the pieces for P2 (player 2) by the number 2, and V (vacant squares) by the number 0.

With these design decisions behind them, Dorothy and Irene can now write P_2, the complete main "program":

P_2 (Refinement of P_1)

global BOARD-STATUS, LEGAL-BLACK-MOVES-MAPPING,
LEGAL-RED-MOVES-MAPPING

PLAYER = BLACK

Square	Left adjacent square	Right adjacent square	Left jump square	Right jump square
BLACK				
1	5	6	—	10
2	6	7	9	11
3	7	8	10	12
4	8	—	11	—
5	—	9	—	14
.	.	.	.	.
.	.	.	.	.
.	.	.	.	.
31	—	—	—	—
32	—	—	—	—
RED				
1	—	—	—	—
2	—	—	—	—
.	.	.	.	.
.	.	.	.	.
.	.	.	.	.
28	24	—	19	—
29	—	25	—	22
30	25	26	21	23
31	26	27	22	24
32	27	28	23	—

Fig. 3.8   Table of legal adjacent squares for each player. Dashes represent illegal moves

```
      OPPONENT = RED
      write (INTRODUCTORY-MESSAGES)

10    input MOVE

      if MOVE is not on board
          then goto 10

      gosub CHECK-LEGAL-MOVE
          using (PLAYER, SQ1, SQ2)
          giving (LEGAL-MOVE-FLAG, CONTINUE-JUMP-FLAG)

      if (LEGAL-MOVE-FLAG is not on)
          then write (ILLEGAL-MOVE-MSG)
                goto 10

        gosub UPDATE-BOARD-STATUS (PLAYER, SQ1, SQ2)
```

if (CONTINUE-JUMP-FLAG is on)
  then gosub CONTINUE-THE-JUMP (PLAYER, SQ2)

if NO-KING-FOR (PLAYER) and MOVES-LEFT-FOR
  (OPPONENT)
  then inform (PLAYER) of completed legal move
     prompt (OPPONENT) for new move
     swap (PLAYER, OPPONENT)
     goto 10

write (WINNING-MSG) for PLAYER
  (LOSING-MSG) for OPPONENT

stop

Although P_2 is in their own notation, Dorothy can now completely formalize P_2 into P_3, which is written in BASIC in Example 3.1.

The Remaining Functions and Subprograms

Now Dorothy takes over the task of specifying each subprogram. Since they are quite straightforward, we will not elaborate on each. We will describe one subprogram to give the reader a feel for operating on the board.

As the sample subprogram, we choose "check-status-of-move." This subroutine takes three arguments: P (Player), S1 (Square 1), and S2 (Square 2). It returns the values of the flags L (Legal-move), J (Jump), and C (Continue-to-jump). (Note: See the section following for an explanation of the J flag.) For a legal move, the following conditions must be met:

1. The moving player must have a piece on S1.
2. S2 must be a left or right adjacent square.
3. S2 must be vacant.
4. If the move is a jump, the intervening square must contain an opponent's piece.
5. If a jump exists for the moving player, the move must not be a nonjump.

One important point must be made. Using the top-down approach, the main program has been so carefully defined and structured that all the procedures cannot be written *independently*. Any subprograms that fit their required definitions for the main program will suffice.

The complete, final program is comprised of the main program and the declaration of all subprograms (see Example 3.2). The reader should go over the main program and subprograms to be satisfied that they work correctly. The reader may have observed several ways of "speeding up" the Kriegspiel program. Efficiency was not a major design criterion in our development, although it could have been. Can you propose several changes to make the program more efficient?

The Real Story of Dorothy and Irene

The above story, with a suitable change of names and places, is by and large accurate. In fact, in writing this chapter, we tried to follow the top-down approach *exactly*. In fairness to you, the reader, we would like to summarize what actually happened.

First, the inputs, outputs, and condition-action mapping underwent many minor revisions as a result of writing the actual program. We consider this a mistake on our part for not meticulously thinking ahead.

Second, we found it important to include a flag for a legal (or nonlegal) jump in the subroutine to check for a legal move. In lower level modules, we found that such a flag was needed. We consider this a serious flaw, for the main program underwent a change that was not anticipated in the original development as given in the text.

Finally, there were debates on the actual kind of error checking performed by the program. This is a difficult area, and the influence of BASIC had some effect on our final decisions.

In parting, we make several comments:

1. We strongly believe in the top-down approach.
2. With any approach, we cannot overemphasize the importance of thinking, and especially, thinking before any code is written.
3. Looking at the final program, which we believe is first-rate, we have noticed a somewhat different, and better, organization. We leave this little exercise to you.

So be it.

Example 3.1 P₃ (Formalized Version of Main Program)

```
1901                 READ P1, P2, V, N
1902            MAT READ I, M1, M2
1903            MAT B = I
1904 REM
1910            LET P = P1
1920            LET O = P2
1930 REM
1940            PRINT #P, 'WELCOME TO KRIEGSPIEL CHECKERS'
1945            PRINT #P, 'ENTER YOUR FIRST MOVE'
1946            PRINT #P, 'XX XX'
1950            PRINT #O, 'WELCOME TO KRIEGSPIEL CHECKERS'
1955            PRINT #O, 'YOUR OPPONENT WILL MAKE THE FIRST MOVE'
1960 REM
1970 REM
1980            INPUT #P, S1, S2
1981            IF ((S1 > 0) AND (S1 < 33))  GOTO 2090
1982            IF ((S2 > 0) AND (S2 < 33))  GOTO 2090
1983              PRINT #P, '***SQUARE(S) OUT OF RANGE***'
1984              PRINT #P, 'TRY AGAIN'
1985              PRINT #P, 'XX XX'
1986              GOTO 1980
2030 REM
2040 REM   ** CHECK FOR LEGAL MOVE
2090            GOSUB 2670
2100 REM
2110            IF (L$ = T$)  GOTO 2180
2120              PRINT #P, 'TRY AGAIN'
2121              PRINT #P, 'XX XX'
2130              GOTO 1980
2140 REM
2150 REM   ** UPDATE THE BOARD
2180            GOSUB 4140
2190 REM
2195 REM   ** CHECK CONTINUABLE-JUMP-FLAG...IF TRUE, PROCESS JUMP
2200            IF (C$ = F$)  GOTO 2290
2260              GOSUB 3000
2270 REM
2280 REM
2290            IF (FNN$ (P) = F$)  GOTO 2390
2300            IF (FNS$ (O) = F$)  GOTO 2390
2310              PRINT #P, 'YOU HAVE COMPLETED A LEGAL MOVE AND'
2315              PRINT #P, 'YOUR OPPONENT HAS BEEN ASKED TO MOVE'
2320              PRINT #O, 'IT IS YOUR TURN TO MOVE'
2321              PRINT #O, 'XX XX'
2330              LET Z = P
2340              LET P = O
2350              LET O = Z
2360              GOTO 1980
2370 REM
2380 REM
2390            PRINT #O, 'SORRY...YOUR OPPONENT HAS WON THE GAME***'
2400            PRINT #P, 'CONGRATULATIONS..YOU HAVE WON THE GAME***'
2410        STOP
```

Example 3.2 Final Program for Kriegspiel Checkers

```
100 REM    **  PROGRAM TITLE      KRIEGSPIEL CHECKERS
110 REM    **
120 REM    **  WRITTEN BY         DR. IRENE B. MALCOM AND DOROTHY E. CLARK
130 REM    **  DATE WRITTEN       SEPTEMBER, 1977
140 REM    **  WRITTEN FOR        COMMISSION ON RECREATIONAL ACTIVITIES,
150 REM    **                     STATE OF ATAD
160 REM
170 REM
180 REM    **  PROGRAM INTENT
190 REM    **      THIS PROGRAM ACTS AS THE REFEREE FOR THE GAME OF
200 REM    **  KRIEGSPIEL CHECKERS AS DEFINED IN THE STATE OF ATAD.
210 REM    **  THE INPUT TO THIS PROGRAM CONSISTS OF A SERIES OF
220 REM    **  MOVES TAKEN FROM TWO INTERACTIVE TERMINALS. THE
230 REM    **  OUTPUT IS THE SEQUENCE OF MESSAGES INFORMING THE
240 REM    **  PLAYERS OF THE CURRENT STATUS OF THE GAME.
250 REM
260 REM
270 REM    **  THERE ARE TWO MAJOR DATA STRUCTURES
280 REM    **   (1)    BOARD GIVES THE STATUS OF EACH OF THE 32 SQUARES
290 REM    **          I.E. WHETHER THE SQUARE IS VACANT, OCCUPIED BY
300 REM    **          PLAYER1, OR OCCUPIED BY PLAYER2.
310 REM
320 REM    **   (2)    MOVES-FOR-PLAYER-1 INDICATES THE POSSIBLE PATHS
330 REM    **          THAT PLAYER 1 CAN TAKE FROM A GIVEN STARTING SQUARE.
340 REM    **          THERE ARE 32 ENTRIES, CORRESPONDING TO THE 32 SQUARES
350 REM    **          ON THE BOARD, AND 4 VALUES PER ENTRY, CORRESPONDING
360 REM    **          TO THE FOUR POSSIBLE PATHS WHICH CAN BE TAKEN FROM
370 REM    **          A GIVEN SQUARE.   THE PATHS ARE DEFINED AS FOLLOWS
380 REM    **              PATH 1...LEFT-ADJACENT
390 REM    **              PATH 2...RIGHT-ADJACENT
400 REM    **              PATH 3...LEFT-JUMP
410 REM    **              PATH 4...RIGHT-JUMP
415 REM    **          MOVES-FOR-PLAYER2 IS DEFINED SIMILARLY.
420 REM
430 REM
440 REM    **  INPUT/OUTPUT FILES
450 REM    **      UNIT 1    I/O DEVICE FOR PLAYER 1
460 REM    **      UNIT 2    I/O DEVICE FOR PLAYER 2
```

Example 3.2 Final Program (Cont'd)

```
530 REM   **   DICTIONARY OF GLOBAL CONSTANTS, VARIABLES, AND FUNCTIONS.
531 REM   **   LOGICAL VARIABLES ARE INDICATED BY A $.
550 REM   **      P....THE CURRENT PLAYER.
551 REM   **      O....THE CURRENT OPPONENT.
552 REM   **      P1...INITIAL VALUE GIVEN TO PLAYER1, BLACK.
560 REM   **      P2...INITIAL VALUE GIVEN TO PLAYER2, RED.
570 REM   **      V....A VACANT SQUARE ON THE PLAYING BOARD.
580 REM   **      N....THE NUMBER OF SQUARES ON THE BOARD.
600 REM   **      I....INITIAL-BOARD, AN ARRAY THAT CONTAINS THE INITIAL
610 REM   **         STATE OF ALL SQUARES (SEE ABOVE).
620 REM   **            I(SQUARE) = 1   ==>   PLAYER1 OCCUPIES SQUARE
630 REM   **            I(SQUARE) = 2   ==>   PLAYER2 OCCUPIES SQUARE
640 REM   **            I(SQUARE) = 0   ==>   SQUARE IS VACANT
641 REM   **      B....BOARD; CURRENT BOARD POSTIONS.
660 REM   **      M1...MOVES-FOR-PLAYER1  (SEE ABOVE).
670 REM   **      M2...MOVES-FOR-PLAYER2  (SEE ABOVE).
671 REM   **      S1...SQUARE1 OF THE CURRENT MOVE.
672 REM   **      S2...SQUARE2 OF THE CURRENT MOVE.
673 REM   **      L$...LEGAL-MOVE-FLAG.
674 REM   **      C$...CONTINUABLE-JUMP-FLAG.
675 REM   **      J$...LEGAL-JUMP-TAKEN-FLAG.
676 REM   **      P0...PATH INDICATED BY A GIVEN MOVE SEQUENCE (SEE BELOW).
677 REM   **      L3...LEFT-ADJACENT PATH.
678 REM   **      R3...RIGHT-ADJACENT PATH.
679 REM   **      L4...LEFT-JUMP PATH.
680 REM   **      R4...RIGHT-JUMP PATH.
681 REM
682 REM   **   FUNCTIONS
683 REM   **      FNN$...NOKING HAS BEEN MADE BY THE OPPONENT.
684 REM   **      FNS$...SQUARE IS VACANT FOR THE PLAYER.
685 REM   **      FNP....PATH-SELECTION FOR THE CURRENT MOVE.
686 REM   **      FNH$...HAS-JUMP AVAILABLE.
687 REM   **      FNL$...LEGAL-JUMP HAS BEEN MADE.
688 REM   **      FNC$...CONTINUABLE-JUMP IS AVAILABLE.
689 REM   **      FNA$...ADJACENT-SQUARE CAN BE OCCUPIED.
690 REM   **      FNJ$...JUMP-SQUARE CAN BE OCCUPIED.
```

Example 3.2 Final Program (Cont'd)

```
691 REM    **   INITIAL VALUES FOR ALL GLOBAL CONSTANTS
700 REM
720        DIM      I(32), M1(32,4), M2(32,4), B(32)
730 REM
750 REM    **      PLAYER1, PLAYER2, VACANT, NUMSQS,   TRUE,    FALSE
760        DATA        1,       2,       0,      32,   'TRUE',  'FALSE'
780 REM
790 REM    **  INITIAL BOARD POSITIONS
800 REM
810        DATA        1,    1,    1,    1
820        DATA        1,    1,    1,    1
830        DATA        1,    1,    1,    1
840        DATA        0,    0,    0,    0
850        DATA        0,    0,    0,    0
860        DATA        2,    2,    2,    2
870        DATA        2,    2,    2,    2
880        DATA        2,    2,    2,    2
890 REM
900 REM
910 REM
920 REM    **  PLAYER1  MOVE TABLE
930 REM
940 REM    **      LEFT...RIGHT....LEFT...RIGHT
950 REM    **      ADJ       ADJ      JMP     JMP
960 REM
970        DATA      5,        6,       0,      10
980        DATA      6,        7,       9,      11
990        DATA      7,        8,      10,      12
1000       DATA      8,        0,      11,       0
1010       DATA      0,        9,       0,      14
1020       DATA      9,       10,      13,      15
1030       DATA     10,       11,      14,      16
1040       DATA     11,       12,      15,       0
1050       DATA     13,       14,       0,      18
1060       DATA     14,       15,      17,      19
1070       DATA     15,       16,      18,      20
1080       DATA     16,        0,      19,       0
1090       DATA      0,       17,       0,      22
1100       DATA     17,       18,      21,      23
1110       DATA     18,       19,      22,      24
1120       DATA     19,       20,      23,       0
1130       DATA     21,       22,       0,      26
1140       DATA     22,       23,      25,      27
1150       DATA     23,       24,      26,      28
1160       DATA     24,        0,      27,       0
1170       DATA      0,       25,       0,      30
1180       DATA     25,       26,      29,      31
1190       DATA     26,       27,      30,      32
1200       DATA     27,       28,      31,       0
1210       DATA     29,       30,       0,       0
1220       DATA     30,       31,       0,       0
1230       DATA     31,       32,       0,       0
1240       DATA     32,        0,       0,       0
1250       DATA      0,        0,       0,       0
1260       DATA      0,        0,       0,       0
1270       DATA      0,        0,       0,       0
1280       DATA      0,        0,       0,       0
```

Example 3.2 Final Program (Cont'd)

```
1320  REM    **   PLAYER2   MOVE TABLE
1330  REM
1340  REM    **        LEFT...RIGHT....LEFT...RIGHT
1350  REM    **        ADJ       ADJ      JMP      JMP
1360  REM
```

		LEFT ADJ	RIGHT ADJ	LEFT JMP	RIGHT JMP
1370	DATA	0,	0,	0,	0
1380	DATA	0,	0,	0,	0
1390	DATA	0,	0,	0,	0
1400	DATA	0,	0,	0,	0
1410	DATA	0,	1,	0,	0
1420	DATA	1,	2,	0,	0
1430	DATA	2,	3,	0,	0
1440	DATA	3,	4,	0,	0
1450	DATA	5,	6,	0,	2
1460	DATA	6,	7,	1,	3
1470	DATA	7,	8,	2,	4
1480	DATA	8,	0,	3,	0
1490	DATA	0,	9,	0,	6
1500	DATA	9,	10,	5,	7
1510	DATA	10,	11,	6,	8
1520	DATA	11,	12,	7,	0
1530	DATA	13,	14,	0,	10
1540	DATA	14,	15,	9,	11
1550	DATA	15,	16,	10,	12
1560	DATA	16,	0,	11,	0
1570	DATA	0,	17,	0,	14
1580	DATA	17,	18,	13,	15
1590	DATA	18,	19,	14,	16
1600	DATA	19,	20,	15,	0
1610	DATA	21,	22,	0,	18
1620	DATA	22,	23,	17,	19
1630	DATA	23,	24,	18,	20
1640	DATA	24,	0,	19,	0
1650	DATA	0,	25,	0,	22
1660	DATA	25,	26,	21,	23
1670	DATA	26,	27,	22,	24
1680	DATA	27,	28,	23,	0

Example 3.2 Final Program (Cont'd)

```
1740 REM    **   MAIN PROGRAM
1750 REM    **   READ INITIAL VALUES OF GLOBAL VARIABLES AND CONSTANTS
1755 REM    **   GIVE PLAYER AND OPPONENT INITIAL VALUES.
1760 REM    **   WELCOME PLAYERS TO THE GAME AND REQUEST THE FIRST MOVE
1770 REM    **   (1980)  READ THE MOVE AND CHECK FOR INPUT ERRORS
1780 REM    **           CHECK FOR LEGALITY OF MOVE
1785 REM    **              USING-  P, S1, S2;  GIVING-  LEGAL-MOVE-FLAG,
1786 REM    **              JUMP-FLAG, CONTINUE-JUMP-FLAG
1790 REM    **           IF ILLEGAL, INFORM THE PLAYER AND RESTART
1800 REM    **   (2180)  IF LEGAL, THEN UPDATE THE BOARD
1810 REM    **           CHECK FOR AND PROCESS A CONTINUABLE JUMP.
1815 REM    **              USING-  P, SQ2
1820 REM    **   (2290)  IF THE PLAYER HAS NOT OBTAINED A KING AND
1830 REM    **           IF THE OPPONENT HAS AT LEAST ONE MOVE AVAILABLE
1840 REM    **           (I)    INFORM THE PLAYER OF A COMPLETED MOVE
1850 REM    **           (II)   ASK THE OPPONENT FOR A NEW MOVE
1860 REM    **           (III)  SWAP PLAYER AND OPPONENT
1870 REM    **           (IV)   RESTART
1880 REM    **   (2390)  ELSE INFORM PLAYERS THAT GAME IS OVER AND STOP
1890 REM
1900 REM
1901             READ P1, P2, V, N, T$, F$
1902        MAT READ I, M1, M2
1903        MAT B = I
1904 REM
1910        LET P = P1
1920        LET O = P2
1930 REM
1940        PRINT #P, 'WELCOME TO KRIEGSPIEL CHECKERS'
1945        PRINT #P, 'ENTER YOUR FIRST MOVE'
1946        PRINT #P, 'XX XX'
1950        PRINT #O, 'WELCOME TO KRIEGSPIEL CHECKERS'
1955        PRINT #O, 'YOUR OPPONENT WILL MAKE THE FIRST MOVE'
1960 REM
1970 REM
1980        INPUT #P, S1, S2
1981        IF ((S1 > 0) AND (S1 < 33))  GOTO 2090
1982        IF ((S2 > 0) AND (S2 < 33))  GOTO 2090
1983          PRINT #P, '***SQUARE(S) OUT OF RANGE***'
1984          PRINT #P, 'TRY AGAIN'
1985          PRINT #P, 'XX XX'
1986          GOTO 1980
```

Example 3.2 Final Program (Cont'd)

```
2030 REM
2040 REM    ** CHECK FOR LEGAL MOVE
2090            GOSUB 2670
2100 REM
2110            IF (L$ = T$)   GOTO 2180
2120                PRINT #P, 'TRY AGAIN'
2121                PRINT #P, 'XX XX'
2130                GOTO 1980
2140 REM
2150 REM    ** UPDATE THE BOARD
2180            GOSUB 4140
2190 REM
2195 REM    ** CHECK CONTINUABLE-JUMP-FLAG...IF TRUE, PROCESS JUMP
2200            IF (C$ = F$)   GOTO 2290
2260                GOSUB 3000
2270 REM
2280 REM
2290            IF (FNN$ (P) = F$)   GOTO 2390
2300            IF (FNS$ (O) = F$)   GOTO 2390
2310                PRINT #P, 'YOU HAVE COMPLETED A LEGAL MOVE AND'
2315                PRINT #P, 'YOUR OPPONENT HAS BEEN ASKED TO MOVE'
2320                PRINT #O, 'IT IS YOUR TURN TO MOVE'
2321                PRINT #O, 'XX XX'
2330                LET Z = P
2340                LET P = O
2350                LET O = Z
2360                GOTO 1980
2370 REM
2380 REM
2390            PRINT #O, 'SORRY..YOUR OPPONENT HAS WON THE GAME***'
2400            PRINT #P, 'CONGRATULATIONS..YOU HAVE WON THE GAME***'
2410        STOP
```

Example 3.2 Final Program (Cont'd)

```
2420 REM
2430 REM    **   LEVEL 2 ROUTINES
2440 REM
2450 REM    **   SUBROUTINE TO CHECK THE STATUS OF THE INPUT MOVE.
2460 REM    **   IT RETURNS THE FOLLOWING FLAGS
2470 REM    **        L$...TRUE IF A LEGAL MOVE HAS BEEN MADE
2480 REM    **        J$...TRUE IF A LEGAL JUMP HAS BEEN MADE
2490 REM    **        C$...TRUE IF A CONTINUABLE JUMP CAN BE MADE.
2500 REM
2510 REM    **   (2670)  INITIALIZE THE FLAGS.
2520 REM    **           VERIFY THAT S1 IS OCCUPIED BY THE PLAYER
2530 REM    **           AND S2 IS VACANT.
2540 REM    **           DETERMINE PATH-TYPE
2550 REM    **           (0)  NO POSSIBLE PATH FROM S1 TO S2
2560 REM    **           (1)  LEFT ADJACENT
2570 REM    **           (2)  RIGHT ADJACENT
2580 REM    **           (3)  LEFT JUMP
2590 REM    **           (4)  RIGHT JUMP
2600 REM    **           IF ADJACENT-TYPE, CHECK FOR A JUMP
2610 REM    **           IF NO JUMP IS POSSIBLE, THEN MOVE IS LEGAL
2620 REM    **   (2840)  IF JUMP-TYPE, THEN
2630 REM    **           (A)  CHECK LEGALITY OF JUMP
2640 REM    **           (B)  CHECK FOR POSSIBLE CONTINUATION
2650 REM
2660 REM
2670            LET L$ = 'FALSE'
2680            LET J$ = 'FALSE'
2690            LET C$ = 'FALSE'
2700 REM
2710 REM
2720            IF ((B(S1) <> P) OR (B(S2) <> V))   GOTO 2890
2730 REM
2740               LET P0 = FNP (P, S1, S2)
2750 REM
2760               IF (P0 = 0)  GOTO 2890
2770               IF ((P0 = 3) OR (P0 = 4))   GOTO 2840
2780 REM
2790               IF (FNH$ (P) = T$)  GOTO 2890
2800                  LET L$ = 'TRUE'
2810                  GOTO 2890
2820 REM
2830 REM
2840               LET J$ = FNL$ (P, S1, P0)
2850               IF (J$ = F$)  GOTO 2890
2860                  LET C$ = FNC$ (P, S2)
2870                  LET L$ = 'TRUE'
2880 REM
2890            RETURN
```

Example 3.2 Final Program (Cont'd)

```
2900 REM    **   SUBROUTINE TO HANDLE JUMP CONTINUATIONS.
2910 REM    **   (3000)   S2 IS USED AS THE INITIAL SQUARE OF THE JUMP
2920 REM    **             THE PLAYER IS ASKED FOR A JUMP CONTINUATION.
2930 REM    **   (3080)   THE MOVE IS CHECKED FOR LEGALITY.
2935 REM    **             USING P, S1, S2  GIVINGLEG-MOV-FLG,
2936 REM    **             JMP-FLG, CONTINUE-JMP-FLG
2940 REM    **             IF THE MOVE IS  NOT LEGAL, A MESSAGE IS PRINTED
2950 REM    **             AND AN ALTERNATE MOVE IS REQUESTED.
2960 REM    **   (3230)   IF THE MOVE IS LEGAL, THE BOARD IS UPDATED.
2961 REM    **             USING P, S1, S2
2970 REM    **          REPEAT (AS NECESSARY) FOR ALL FURTHER JUMPS.
2980 REM
2990 REM
3000             LET S1 = S2
3010             PRINT #P, 'YOUR JUMP MUST BE CONTINUED'
3015             PRINT #P, 'ENTER JUMP SQUARE'
3016             PRINT #P, 'XX'
3020 REM
3030 REM
3080             INPUT P#, S2
3081             IF ((S1 > 0) AND (S1 < 33))  GOTO 3160
3082                PRINT #P, '***SQUARE OUT OF RANGE***'
3083                PRINT #P, 'TRY AGAIN'
3084                PRINT #P, 'XX'
3085                GOTO 3080
3090 REM
3100 REM
3110 REM    ** MOVE IS CHECKED FOR LEGALITY
3160             GOSUB 2670
3170 REM
3180             IF (J$ = T$)  GOTO 3230
3190                PRINT #P, 'ILLEGAL JUMP CONTINUATION'
3200                PRINT #P, 'TRY AGAIN'
3201                PRINT #P, 'XX'
3210                GOTO 3080
3220 REM
3225 REM    ** UPDATE THE BOARD TO INDICATE THE JUMP
3230             GOSUB 4140
3240 REM
3250             IF (C$ = T$)  GOTO 3000
3260 REM
3270 REM
3280             RETURN
```

Example 3.2 Final Program (Cont'd)

```
3290 REM    **  FUNCTION RETURNS TRUE IF THE PLAYER HAS NOT
3300 REM    **  MOVED A PIECE TO THE OPPONENT'S BACK COURT
3310 REM
3320       DEF FNN$ (P)
3330 REM
3340          LET FNN$ = 'FALSE'
3350 REM
3360          IF (P = P2)  GOTO 3460
3370 REM
3380             IF (B(29) = P1)  GOTO 3530
3390             IF (B(30) = P1)  GOTO 3530
3400             IF (B(31) = P1)  GOTO 3530
3410             IF (B(32) = P1)  GOTO 3530
3420                LET FNN$ = 'TRUE'
3430                GOTO 3530
3440 REM
3450 REM
3460             IF (B(1) = P2)  GOTO 3530
3470             IF (B(2) = P2)  GOTO 3530
3480             IF (B(3) = P2)  GOTO 3530
3490             IF (B(4) = P2)  GOTO 3530
3500                LET FNN$ = 'TRUE'
3510 REM
3520 REM
3530          FNEND
```

Example 3.2 Final Program (Cont'd)

```
3550 REM    **  FUNCTION RETURNS TRUE IF THERE IS A SQUARE FREE FOR
3551 REM    **  THE PLAYER.
3560 REM    **  (3720)  FIND A SQUARE WHICH IS OCCUPIED BY THE PLAYER
3570 REM    **  (3780)  DETERMINE ALL PATHS EMANATING FROM THAT SQUARE
3580 REM    **          (FOR EITHER PLAYER)
3590 REM    **  (3920)  CHECK FOR AN ADJACENT SQUARE FREE.
3600 REM    **          IF NOT, THEN CHECK FOR A JUMP SQUARE FREE
3610 REM    **          REPEAT SEARCH UNTIL EITHER
3620 REM    **          (I)   A FREE SQUARE IS FOUND OR
3630 REM    **          (II)  ALL SQUARES HAVE BEEN CHECKED
3640 REM
3650        DEF FNS$ (P)
3660 REM
3670 REM
3680            LET FNS$ = 'FALSE'
3690 REM
3700            LET S0 = 1
3710 REM
3720            IF (B(S0) = P)  GOTO 3780
3730                LET S0 = S0 + 1
3740                IF (S0 ≥ N)  GOTO 4020
3750                GOTO 3720
3760 REM
3770 REM
3780            IF (P = P2)  GOTO 3860
3790                LET L3 = M1(S0,1)
3800                LET R3 = M1(S0,2)
3810                LET L4 = M1(S0,3)
3820                LET R4 = M1(S0,4)
3830                GOTO 3920
3840 REM
3850 REM
3860                LET L3 = M2(S0,1)
3870                LET R3 = M2(S0,2)
3880                LET L4 = M2(S0,3)
3890                LET R4 = M2(S0,4)
3900 REM
3910 REM
3920            LET FNS$ = FNA$ (L3, R3)
3930            IF (FNS$ = T$)  GOTO 4020
3940                LET FNS$ = FNJ$ (O,L3, L4, R3, R4)
3950 REM
3960 REM
3970            IF ((FNS$ = T$) OR (S0 > N))  GOTO 4020
3980                LET S0 = S0 + 1
3990                GOTO 3720
4000 REM
4010 REM
4020            FNEND
```

Example 3.2 Final Program (Cont'd)

```
4040 REM    **  SUBROUTINE TO CHANGE THE STATE OF THE BOARD FOR THE
4041 REM    **  CURRENT MOVE.
4050 REM    **  (4140)  S1 IS SET VACANT
4060 REM    **          S2 IS SET TO PLAYER
4070 REM    **  IF A JUMP WAS MADE, SET THE JUMPED SQUARE VACANT
4080 REM    **  (CODE IS INCLUDED FOR EITHER PLAYER)
4090 REM    **          IF PATH WAS LEFT-JUMP,
4100 REM    **          THEN SET LEFT-ADJACENT SQUARE VACANT
4110 REM    **  (4240)  IF PATH WAS RIGHT-JUMP,
4120 REM    **          THEN SET RIGHT-ADJACENT SQUARE VACANT
4130 REM
4140            LET B(S1) = V
4150            LET B(S2) = P
4160 REM
4170            IF (P = P2)  GOTO 4300
4180 REM
4190                IF (M1(S1,3) <> S2)  GOTO 4240
4200                LET B(M1(S1,1)) = V
4210                GOTO 4400
4220 REM
4230 REM
4240                IF (M1(S1,4) <> S2)  GOTO 4400
4250                LET B(M1(S1,2)) = V
4260                GOTO 4400
4270 REM
4280 REM
4290 REM
4300                IF (M2(S1,3) <> S2)  GOTO 4350
4310                LET B(M2(S1,1)) = V
4320                GOTO 4400
4330 REM
4340 REM
4350                IF (M2(S1,4) <> S2)  GOTO 4400
4360                LET B(M2(S1,2)) = V
4370 REM
4380 REM
4390 REM
4400        RETURN
```

Example 3.2 Final Program (Cont'd)

```
4410 REM    **    LEVEL3 ROUTINES
4420 REM
4430 REM    **    FUNCTION RETURNS TRUE IF THE BOARD IS VACANT
4431 REM    **    AT EITHER OF THE TWO INPUT SQUARES.
4440 REM    **           CHECK WHETHER LEFT-ADJACENT SQUARE IS LEGAL
4450 REM    **           RETURN TRUE IF THE BOARD IS FREE AT THAT LOCATION.
4460 REM    **    (4610)  CHECK WHETHER RIGHT-ADJACENT SQUARE IS LEGAL
4470 REM    **           RETURN TRUE IF THE BOARD IS FREE AT THAT LOCATION.
4480 REM
4490        DEF FNA$ (L3, R3)
4500 REM
4510 REM
4520           LET FNA$ = 'FALSE'
4530 REM
4540           IF (L3 = 0)  GOTO 4610
4550 REM
4560              IF (B(L3) <> V)  GOTO 4660
4570                 LET FNA$ = 'TRUE'
4580                 GOTO 4660
4590 REM
4600 REM
4610           IF (R3 = 0)  GOTO 4660
4620              IF (B(R3) <> V)  GOTO 4660
4630                 LET FNA$ = 'TRUE'
4640 REM
4650 REM
4660           FNEND
```

Example 3.2 Final Program (Cont'd)

```
4680 REM    **  FUNCTION RETURNS TRUE IF THE PLAYER HAS A JUMP.
4690 REM    **  (4840)   FIND A SQUARE WHICH IS OCCUPIED BY THE PLAYER
4700 REM    **  (4900)   DETERMINE ALL PATHS EMANATING FROM THAT SQUARE
4710 REM    **            (FOR EITHER PLAYER)
4720 REM    **  (5040)   CHECK FOR A JUMP
4730 REM    **            CONTINUE PROCESSING UNTIL EITHER
4740 REM    **            (I)   A FREE SQUARE IS FOUND OR
4750 REM    **            (II)  ALL SQUARES HAVE BEEN CHECKED
4760 REM
4770        DEF FNH$(P)
4780 REM
4790 REM
4800            LET FNH$ = 'FALSE'
4810 REM
4820            LET S0 = 1
4830 REM
4840            IF (B(S0) = P)  GOTO 4900
4850                LET S0 = S0 + 1
4860                IF (S0 > N)  GOTO 5160
4870                GOTO 4840
4880 REM
4890 REM
4900            IF (P = P2)  GOTO 4980
4910                LET L3 = M1(S0,1)
4920                LET R3 = M1(S0,2)
4930                LET L4 = M1(S0,3)
4940                LET R4 = M1(S0,4)
4950                GOTO 5040
4960 REM
4970 REM
4980                LET L3 = M2(S0,1)
4990                LET R3 = M2(S0,2)
5000                LET L4 = M2(S0,3)
5010                LET R4 = M2(S0,4)
5020 REM
5030 REM
5040            LET FNH$ = FNJ$(0, L3, L4, R3, R4)
5050 REM
5060 REM
5070            IF (FNH$ = T$)  GOTO 5130
5080            IF (S0 >= N)      GOTO 5160
5090                LET S0 = S0 + 1
5100                GOTO 4840
5110 REM
5120 REM
5130            PRINT #P, 'A JUMP IS AVAILABLE AND YOU MUST TAKE IT'
5140 REM
5150 REM
5160        FNEND
```

Example 3.2 Final Program (Cont'd)

```
5180  REM     **    FUNCTION RETURNS TRUE IF A JUMP IS LEGAL.
5190  REM     **            S3 CONTAINS THE LOCATION OF THE SQUARE TO BE JUMPED.
5200  REM     **   (5360)   THE LOCATION IS OCCUPIED BY THE OPPONENT, THEREFORE
5210  REM     **            INFORM THE OPPONENT OF A CAPTURED SQUARE.
5220  REM
5230  REM
5240          DEF FNL$ (P, S1, P0)
5250  REM
5260  REM
5270             LET FNL$ = 'FALSE'
5280  REM
5290             IF (P = P2)  GOTO 5330
5300                LET S3 = M1(S1,P0-2)
5310                GOTO 5360
5320  REM
5330                LET S3 = M2(S1,P0-2)
5340  REM
5350  REM
5360             IF (B(S3) <> 0)  GOTO 5410
5370                PRINT #0, 'PIECE CAPTURED FROM SQUARE'; S3
5380                LET FNL$ = 'TRUE'
5390  REM
5400  REM
5410          FNEND
```

Example 3.2 Final Program (Cont'd)

```
5430 REM    **   FUNCTION RETURNS TRUE IF A JUMP CAN BE CONTINUED.
5440 REM    **        LOOK AHEAD AT THE SQUARES BEYOND THE CURRENT MOVE.
5450 REM    **   (5660)   ALLOWABLE MOVES MUST EXIST ALONG EITHER THE
5460 REM    **            LEFT-JUMP PATH OR THE RIGHT-JUMP PATH.
5470 REM
5480 REM
5490        DEF FNC$ (P, S2)
5500 REM
5510 REM
5520            IF (P = P2)   GOTO 5600
5530                LET L3 = M1(S2,1)
5540                LET R3 = M1(S2,2)
5550                LET L4 = M1(S2,3)
5560                LET R4 = M1(S2,4)
5570                GOTO 5660
5580 REM
5590 REM
5600                LET L3 = M2(S2,1)
5610                LET R3 = M2(S2,2)
5620                LET L4 = M2(S2,3)
5630                LET R4 = M2(S2,4)
5640 REM
5650 REM
5660            LET FNC$ = FNJ$ (O, L3, L4, R3, R4)
5670 REM
5680 REM
5690        FNEND
```

Example 3.2 Final Program (Cont'd)

```
5710 REM    **   FUNCTION TO RETURN A VALUE INDICATING
5720 REM    **   (0)   ILLEGAL PATH,
5730 REM    **   (1)   LEFT-ADJACENT PATH,
5740 REM    **   (2)   RIGHT-ADJACENT PATH,
5750 REM    **   (3)   LEFT-JUMP,
5760 REM    **   (4)   RIGHT-JUMP.
5770 REM
5775 REM         (CODE IS PROVIDED FOR EITHER PLAYER)
5780 REM    **   THE MOVES-FOR-PLAYER1 (OR MOVES-FOR-PLAYER2) TABLE
5790 REM    **   IS REFERENCED.  AN ATTEMPT IS MADE TO MATCH S2
5800 REM    **   WITH ANY OF THE ROW ENTRIES OF THE COLUMN INDEXED BY
5810 REM    **   S1.  THE ROW OF THE MATCHING ENTRY IS RETURNED.
5820 REM
5830 REM
5840        DEF FNP (P, S1, S2)
5850 REM
5860 REM
5870           LET FNP = 0
5880 REM
5890           FOR P0 = 1 TO 4
5900             IF (P = P2)  GOTO 5950
5910               IF (M1(S1,P0) <> S2)   GOTO 5980
5920                  LET FNP = P0
5930                  GOTO 6010
5940 REM
5950               IF (M2(S1,P0) <> S2)   GOTO 5980
5960                  LET FNP = P0
5970                  GOTO 6010
5980           NEXT P0
5990 REM
6000 REM
6010        FNEND
```

Example 3.2 Final Program (Cont'd)

```
6030 REM
6040 REM    **   LEVEL 4 ROUTINE
6050 REM
6060 REM    **   FUNCTION RETURNS TRUE IF EITHER OF THE TWO INPUT
6070 REM    **   PATHS CORRESPOND TO A LEGAL JUMP
6080 REM    **   (I)     ADJACENT AND JUMP SQUARES MUST BE ON THE BOARD
6090 REM    **   (II)    ADJACENT SQUARE MUST BE OCCUPIED BY OPPONENT
6100 REM    **   (III)   JUMP SQUARE MUST BE VACANT
6110 REM    **   (CODE FOR BOTH PLAYERS IS SUPPLIED)
6120 REM
6130 REM
6140        DEF FNJ$ (O, L3, L4, R3, R4)
6150 REM
6160 REM
6170           LET FNJ$ = 'FALSE'
6180 REM
6190           IF ((L3 = 0) OR (L4 = 0))  GOTO 6250
6200              IF ((B(L3) <> O) OR (B(L4) <> V))   GOTO 6300
6210                 LET FNJ$ = 'TRUE'
6220                 GOTO 6300
6230 REM
6240 REM
6250           IF ((R3 = 0) OR (R4 = 0))  GOTO 6300
6260              IF ((B(&3) <> O) OR (B(R4) <> V))   GOTO 6300
6270                 LET FNJ$ = 'TRUE'
6280 REM
6290 REM
6300        FNEND
6310        END
```

EXERCISES

Exercise 3.1   (Programming Proverbs)
List three ways in which Irene and Dorothy followed the proverb, "Don't Leave the Reader in the Dust."

Exercise 3.2   (Programming Approaches)
Write a short position paper comparing the "top-down" approach with the "systems analyst" approach of Chapter 2.

Exercise 3.3   (The Input/Output Mapping)
Develop an alternative to the condition-action list method for expressing how a program is to map input situations to output responses. Consider a decision table approach.

Exercise 3.4   (Program Levels)
Draw a complete tree in the form of Fig. 3.2 to illustrate the levels of the Kriegspiel program.

Exercise 3.5   (Writing the Levels of a Given Program)
Write a sequence of levels that might have been used to generate the program in the prettyprint proverb.

Exercise 3.6   (Program Modification)
Modify the Kriegspiel program to accept moves in a completely free format, that is, without requiring column placement of the two squares.

Exercise 3.7   (Program Critique)
List five parts of the Kriegspiel program that, from a quality point of view, can be improved.

Exercise 3.8   (Speeding Up a Program)
Discuss five different ways for speeding up the Kriegspiel program. If you had to pick one way, which would cause the greatest speed-up?

Exercise 3.9   (Program Development)
Write both an informal and formal statement of the P_3 module "check-status-of-move" for the Kriegspiel program.

Exercise 3.10   (Program Development)
Following the same specification and top-down development strategy as Irene's, present a complete program to solve the following problem:

> *Input:*   A sequence of characters representing the text of a letter. The text contains only alphabetic English words, blanks, commas,

periods, and the special word "PP" denoting the beginning of a paragraph.

Output: 1. The number of words in the text.
2. The text given as input, printed according to the following format:
   a. The first line of each paragraph is to be indented five spaces and successive lines are to be left-adjusted. Lines are printed in units of 60 or fewer characters.
   b. One blank is to separate each word from the previous word, comma, or period.
   c. A word cannot be broken across lines.

Exercise 3.11   (Programming Pressure)
Will Irene take over Mr. Coleman's job?

CHAPTER FOUR
PROGRAM STANDARDS

"Any programmer who fails to comply with the standard naming, formatting or commenting conventions should be shot. If it so happens that it is inconvenient to shoot him, then he is to be politely requested to recode his program in adherence to the above standard."

Michael Spier [Ref. S1]

The BASIC language has been with us since 1965, yet the writing of high-quality BASIC programs has remained a matter of personal style. The thrust of this chapter is to go beyond the "proverbs" and present some rigorous standards for the writing of BASIC programs. Developing rigorous program standards is not easy, for the rules must be unambiguous, of sufficient merit so that a programmer will not be unduly stifled by their adoption, and ideally, machine testable. We have followed this chapter's program standards throughout this book.

The importance of developing such standards is clear. For managers, instructors, and programmers, there is a need to develop uniform rules so that everyone may more easily understand programs, a need to develop coding techniques that reduce the complexity of programs, and a need to control the entire software development effort.

We make no attempt here to encompass every feature of the BASIC language. No standard can attempt to cover every aspect of a given programming problem. Nevertheless, the standards presented in this book should go a long way to promote quality programs.

GENERAL REQUIREMENTS

[GEN-1]   *Any violation of the program standards must be approved by someone appointed to enforce the standards.*

The rationale here is to allow exceptions to the program standards, but *only* if a responsible agent gives approval. It is critical that all program standards, unless revoked, be followed to the very last detail. The method for enforcing the standards is left to the particular instructor or manager.

[GEN-2] *Each installation shall have established alignment (prettyprinting) conventions.*

The rationale here is also to promote readability and to save time by once and for all developing a fixed set of rules. The value of adopting rules for good program spacing is enormous. The tedium involved in alignment can be offset by an (automatic) formatting program. A specific set of alignment rules is given in Appendix B.

[GEN-3] *No program unit may exceed two pages of code.*

The rationale here is to force program units (i.e., main programs, functions, or subroutines) to be isolated on two pages of text at most. In general, each program unit should occupy no more than a single page of text. However, due to the frequent exceptional cases where initializations or repeated computations require extensive code, the standard allows program units to occupy up to two pages of text.

[GEN-4] *All programs shall include the following comment:*

```
REM    **    PROGRAM TITLE      Brief title
REM    **
REM    **    WRITTEN BY         Name of author(s)
REM    **    DATE WRITTEN       Date of first execution
REM    **    WRITTEN FOR        Responsible unit
REM    **
REM    **    PROGRAM INTENT     Brief program summary
                     .                    .
                     .                    .
REM    **    INPUT FILES
                  file-name          Brief description of use
                     .                    .
                     .                    .
REM    **    OUTPUT FILES
REM    **       file-name           Brief description of use
                     .                    .
                     .                    .
```

The rationale here is to give a quick synopsis of the program's intent, input and output files, and title information, so that a program has some minimal internal documentation.

DATA STATEMENTS

[DATA-1]   *DATA statements used to initialize constants must appear before the first executable statement.*

[DATA-2]   *DATA statements used to initialize nonfile oriented input variables must appear after the END statement.*

The rationale here is to distinguish constant values from input values.

[DATA-3]   *All numeric values, character strings, and arrays that remain constant throughout a program must be given a name and a value in a DATA statement.*

[DATA-4]   *No variable (i.e., one whose value is changed in an executable statement) may be initialized in a DATA statement.*

The rationale of [DATA-3] is to isolate constants in a DATA statement and, if need be, to allow changes without affecting the logic in the executable statements. The rationale of [DATA-4] is to require initialization of variables in the statements that change the values of the variables. The overall rationale is to draw a clear line between names for "constants" and "variables."

For example, use

```
10      DATA 100, 0.001
20      READ N, E
30      LET H = 0
40      FOR I = 1 TO N
50          IF (A(I) >= E) GOTO 70
60              LET H = H + 1
70      NEXT I
```

rather than

```
10      LET H = 0
20      FOR I = 1 TO 100
30          IF (A(I) >= 0.001) GOTO 50
40              LET H = H +1
50      NEXT I
```

or

```
10      DATA 0
20      READ H
30      LET E = 0.001
```

```
40      FOR I = 1 TO N
50          IF (A(I) >= E) GOTO 70
60              LET H = H + 1
70      NEXT I
```

CONTROL STRUCTURES

[CNTRL-1]   *GOTO statements may be used only in the following forms. Any of the following statement sequences may be null, and the statement label moved accordingly.*

(a) ℓ_1 IF (logical-expression) GOTO ℓ_2
              statement-sequence$_1$
              GOTO ℓ_1
       ℓ_2 statement-sequence$_2$

(b) ℓ_1 statement-sequence$_1$
              IF (logical-expression) GOTO ℓ_2
              statement-sequence$_2$
              GOTO ℓ_1
       ℓ_2 statement-sequence$_3$

(c)   IF (logical-expression) GOTO ℓ_1
              statement-sequence$_1$
              GOTO ℓ_2
       ℓ_1 statement-sequence$_2$
       ℓ_2 statement-sequence$_3$

(d)   ON (numeric-expression) ℓ_1, ℓ_2, ℓ_3
       ℓ_1 statement-sequence$_1$
              GOTO ℓ_4
       ℓ_2 statement-sequence$_2$
              GOTO ℓ_4
       ℓ_3 statement-sequence$_3$
       ℓ_4 statement-sequence$_4$

The rationale here is to force the programmers to *think ahead* and use only 1-in, 1-out control structures. Many programmers at first believe that this restriction is unreasonable. With some practice, programming with these control structures becomes quite easy. If it seems necessary to use a GOTO in another setting, the following alternatives should be considered:

1. Restructuring the algorithm
2. Putting blocks of code in a subroutine
3. Copying in a piece of code
4. Repeating a condition previously tested
5. Reversing a condition to its negative.

[CNTRL-2]   *STOP and RETURN statements may only be used as the last executable statement of a main program, function, or subroutine.*

The rationale here is to force a complete use of 1-in, 1-out control structures and to make the logical exit of a program identical to its lexical end.

[CNTRL-3]   *FOR-loop variables may not be assigned a new value within the range of the FOR-loop and may not be used after execution of the FOR-loop without reinitializing its value.*

The rationale here is to prevent clever but deceptive loop controls.

[CNTRL-4]   *GOTO statements may not be used to transfer control to a nonexecutable statement.*

Although BASIC allows control to be transferred to such statements as REM, DIM, etc., this would obscure the underlying logic.

DIMENSION STATEMENTS

[DIM-1]   *All DIM statements in a module must be placed before the first executable statement.*

[DIM-2]   *All arrays must be explicitly dimensioned.*

The rationale here is to isolate and specify all data structures clearly.

FUNCTIONS

[FUN-1]   *All single line functions in a module must be placed before the first executable statement.*

The rationale here is to isolate the function. The function definition should be treated as if it were a specification statement and thus it should be placed at the beginning of a module.

[FUN-2]   *A global variable may not be used in an expression referencing a function which uses that variable.*

The BASIC interpreter cannot handle this situation and gives unpredictable results.

[FUN-3]   *The formal parameters of a function may not be assigned new values within the body of the function.*

The rationale here is to provide a model for functions as mappings from input values into a (single) returned value. Since BASIC does not allow local variables, side effects can still occur. The programmer should effectively create local variables by using unique names in the function body.

OTHER CONSTRUCTS

[OTHER-1]   *Parentheses must be used to specify the order of evaluation for the components of compound logical expressions.*

The rationale here is to make arithmetic and logical operations more visible and not to rely on the sometimes confusing left-to-right or precedence rules. For example,

$$L \; OR \; A + B >= C$$

is to be written

$$L \; OR \; ((A + B) >= C)$$

[OTHER-2]   *All INPUT variables must be checked for errors upon data entry.*

The rationale here is to aid in program correctness/verification.

[OTHER-3]   *Array structures may not be reformulated.*

BASIC allows implicit redimensioning of arrays. For example,

$$DIM \; A(10)$$

.

.

.

$$LET \; A(3,3) = 0$$

is allowed. This clearly confuses the meaning of the data structure. Create another array!

[OTHER-4]   *All variables must be explicitly initialized before they are used on the right side of a LET statement.*

The rationale here is to ensure that the programmer explicitly initializes all variables and constants. In particular, it is not permissible to assume that the interpreter will initialize variables to 0.

CONCLUSIONS

The general issue of program standards is indeed complex. When an attempt is made to restrict the initial boundaries of a language, the programmer resistance can be great. In addition, any attempt to promote or enforce such a set of program standards must resolve a number of difficult issues.

First, exceptional cases must be avoided when writing a standard. It is critical that the standard be as solid as possible, for, otherwise, the credibility of the entire activity can be undermined. Possible exceptional cases must thus be carefully screened before the standard is adopted.

Second, there is the issue of enforcement. What mechanism should be set up to enforce the standards? Can the standards really be enforced without some kind of automatic aids? What about the programmer who does not see any reason for a particular standard or its use in a particular case? These questions are difficult to answer.

Third, given that some method of enforcement has been adopted and given that some useful exception does occur, how is the exception to be handled? While an ideal standard has no exceptions, when exceptions do arise, they have to be handled without undermining the credibility of the entire effort.

Fourth, there are a number of human factors that must be faced, especially when standards are being developed. For one, choices may be a matter of taste, and there are bound to be some arbitrary decisions. Further, there may be some initial overhead in following the standards. The human tendency is to get on with the job, i.e., code. This tendency must be resisted, for if the standards are correct, breaking the standards is shortsighted.

Finally, one must be very careful to avoid expecting too much from the standards, for eventually the problem-dependent features of a program will demand special attention. While the adoption of good standards may help in producing good solutions to the problem at hand, ultimately the style and expertise of the practicing programmer will become paramount.

CHAPTER FIVE

ODDS AND ENDS

THE OVERCONCERN WITH MICROEFFICIENCY

Machine efficiency has been one of the most frequent concerns of managers, instructors, and programmers alike. In the early years of computing, when hardware configurations were small and slow, it was important to use as little storage space or computer time as possible. Since then, digital computers have become larger, less expensive, and considerably faster. Yet there is still frequent concern with the question of machine efficiency because of the need to control programming costs.

The reasons for striving for machine efficiency are not only historic and economic; there is also a certain human element. Programmers take pride in their ability to squeeze out excess lines of code or to use an appropriate efficiency feature, and managers take a natural pride in the speed of their programs or their compact use of storage.

The Real Costs

While we do not at all question the need to reduce programming costs, we do believe that this concern is often focused on the wrong issues. For example, some typical concerns in BASIC programming are the following:

1. Avoiding poor quality (or excessive reduction of) commands.
2. Avoiding subroutines and functions.
3. Making liberal use of GOTOs.
4. Writing IF statements so that the most frequent conditions are checked first.
5. Writing "powerful" one-line expressions.
6. Making multiple uses of a single name.

These objectives are meant to save space and execution time, thus lowering costs. Because of the often rather small and local savings afforded by the above techniques, we shall call the efficiency they provide "microefficiency" [Ref. A1]. With the development of inexpensive fast storage and larger memory systems, the preoccupation with the size and speed of machine code would seem to have been dealt a death blow. Not so! Old habits remain.

The concern with microefficiency has often obscured the really important programming costs. The first issue is to understand the problem completely and make sure that the resulting specification satisfies the user. The second issue is to produce high-quality system design, clear code, and clear documentation. The final issue, and only if necessary, is to produce a fast or compact program.

While microefficient programs do help to reduce overall costs, in the larger perspective, they are usually only a small factor. The total cost of a system includes the costs of promotion, time needed to understand user requirements, the development of clear and acceptable specifications, program writing, documentation, and above all, maintenance. If a proposed programming system is not acceptable to the ultimate user, further development is wasted. If specifications are not adequate, system development is often misdirected and delayed. If there is a failure to recognize exceptional conditions and different solution strategies or if there is a poor initial design, the success of any development effort is undermined. Moreover, program development costs include programmer training, thinking time, coding time, and the time and effort needed to integrate a subsystem into an overall system. Documentation costs include the time needed to prepare reports, figures, and summaries of existing code.

In the life of many large programs, the largest cost factor is system maintenance. Maintenance of an ill-conceived, poorly developed, poorly coded, or poorly documented system is expensive and time consuming at best. More typically, program performance is seriously degraded. Easy maintenance of itself can yield greater savings than microefficient program performance. To control programming costs, we must look in the right places.

Program Performance

There are, of course, cases where the costs of program performance are significant. Perhaps a given program will be run every day, a given data file may be accessed every hour, or fast memory may be scarce. In these cases, attention should be devoted to the *top* levels of program design where "macroefficient" techniques can be applied.

It does little good to scatter time and space microefficiencies all over the code if the file and array organizations are not optimal. At an even higher level, file and array techniques will be of little avail if the entire program frequently needs to be restarted because of the errors due to the improper input of data. In such cases, perhaps several sequentially executed programs with local and less severe restraints should be designed and substituted for one large program. At the highest level, if the whole program is more easily handled without a digital computer, all the concern with computer performance cost is meaningless.

A rather significant issue stems from the following observation. It is estimated that 90 percent of the CPU time in a program is spent on 10 percent of the code. If a programmer is faced with program performance demands, the first consideration should be *where* the program is losing its time. Microefficiency can then be spent on this 10 percent of the code.

Finally, if a program is designing low-level portions of code and really needs microefficient techniques, caution is still in order. Considerations such as parking characters in integer values or avoiding character types can make a program quite machine dependent. Tight, tricky, microefficient code can be almost impossible for another person to understand. These performance savings may in the end raise the cost of program maintenance.

The overriding points of our discussion can be summarized as follows. The concern with program microefficiency is often shortsighted. The primary concern should be to consider overall program costs and to place major economic emphasis on earlier phases of program development. There is a lot of money being wasted in the production of poor definitions, poor designs, poor documentation, and in the development of slipshod programs.

THE CASE AGAINST PROGRAM FLOWCHARTS

In 1947, H. H. Goldstine and J. von Neumann [Ref. G1] introduced a pictorial notation called a "flow diagram." Its purpose was to facilitate the translation of algorithms into machine language programs. The flow diagrams pictured the course of machine control through a sequence of steps and indicated the contents and change of items in storage. Since then these ideas and notations, along with various diagrams and charts used in business system analysis [Ref. C4], have been absorbed into almost all areas of electronic data processing. The basic concept has come to be known as "flowcharting." We can roughly distinguish between two types of flowcharts: system flowcharts and program flowcharts.

System flowcharts describe the flow of major data items and the control sequence of major operations in an information-processing system. It is customary to picture the relationship existing between information, media, equipment, equipment operations, and manual operations. An example is given in Fig. 5.1. There are few specific details, and only a rough picture of the overall process. As with document flowcharts, system flowcharts concentrate more on the flow of data than on the flow of control.

Program flowcharts specify details of the sequential flow of control through an actual program. A familiar example is Fig. 5.2. Program flowcharts are the most direct descendant of Goldstine and von Neumann's flow diagrams, for both describe the flow of control in great detail. It is interesting to note that program flowcharts do not explicitly describe the data flow, as was the case with the original flow diagrams.

As for system flowcharts, we believe that they can be useful aids in describing systems and processes. For documentation, system flowcharts can

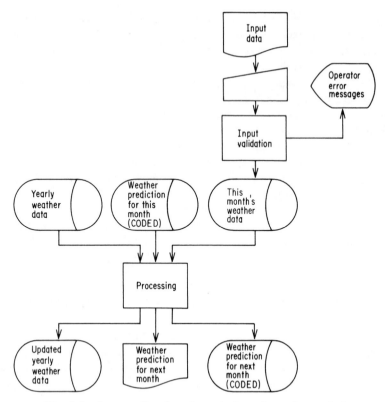

Fig. 5.1   A system flowchart for end-of-month weather analysis

give a quick synopsis of a process. Unfortunately, the use of these flowcharts has sometimes been mistaken for complete problem description.

Our concern here is with program flowcharts, a technique familiar to all programmers and one often used daily. It is perhaps true that program flowcharts can assist in the design of very efficient, small algorithms. However, we believe that program flowcharts can easily suppress much useful information in favor of highlighting sequential control flow, something which distracts the programmer from the important functional relationship in the overall design. This in turn may obscure the use of alternative designs via the use of procedures and subprograms, the use of more intuitive data structures, or even the simple fine tuning of logic.

Consider the program flowchart schema in Fig. 5.3. The a_i stand for certain actions (e.g., assignments or subroutine calls); the d_i stand for decisions. The programmer who derived this flowchart was so concerned with lines and boxes (i.e., sequences of steps) that the resulting code, while correct, tended to obscure the overall functional logic.

Other design methods resulted in a different solution, which was not as

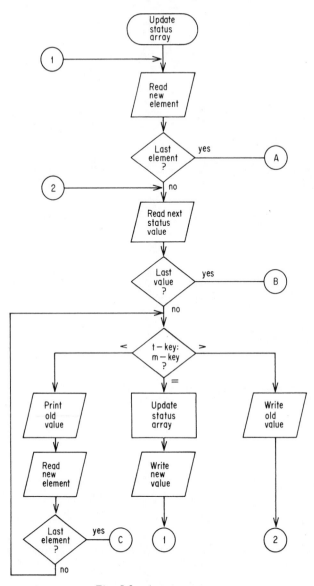

Fig. 5.2 A strange program

brief as that obtained from program flowcharts, but easier to understand. Figure 5.4 pictures the control flow derived from this new code.

One important problem with program flowcharts is keeping track of variables that change from one part of the flowchart to the next. A user who is preoccupied with flow of control details may quickly be in the position of the tourist to Boston who decides to drive his own car to see the sights. By not taking

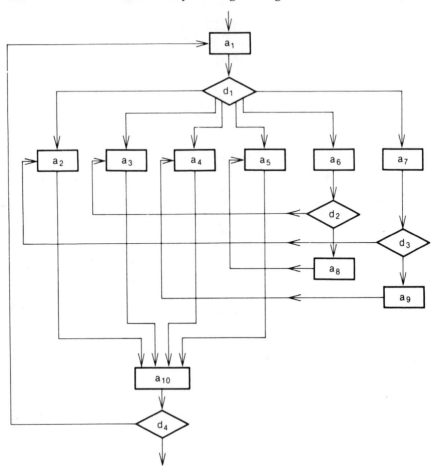

Fig. 5.3   A program flowchart schema

a sight-seeing bus, the visitor quickly gets distracted in the confusion of alternative routes.

Thinking back, were you ever asked to update or correct a program in which the documentation included program flowcharts? How often did you utilize them? Our observations indicate little such use of the charts. In the majority of cases the use of program flowcharts is replaced by a careful study of the code that produced them in the first place. Good code alone seems to be sufficient for the detailed understanding needed for program maintenance.

Program flowcharts have less severe deficiencies. One is a general untidiness caused by the simple human limitation in the art of drawing straight lines and figures, which makes flowcharting a time-consuming activity as well. Also, who in tarnation borrowed my template?

Besides its somewhat awkward notation, did you ever notice that a pro-

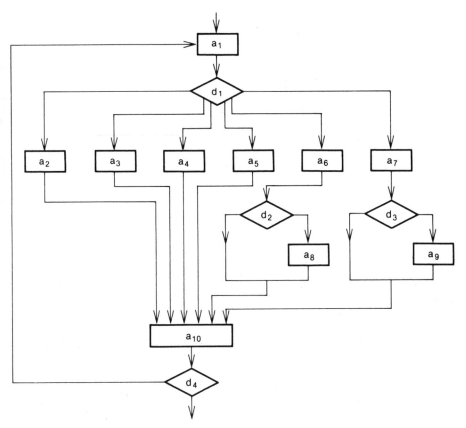

Fig. 5.4   Program flowchart schema derived from alternative code

gram flowchart always seems to spill over the margin of the paper used to draw it on? Look back at Figure 5.2. This flowchart requires numerous connectors and page skipping to read the result. After reading a few pages, who knows where you came from, never mind where you are going. Even if you manage to keep connectors to a minimum to prevent mental page flipping, data processing still involves many conditional checks (i.e., branches) in flowcharts. When you connect all these branches to their logical destinations, you may see what is known as the "spaghetti effect," which is a profusion of crisscrossing branches.

Because of the rather large amount of time and work required to construct program flowcharts, program designers are naturally reluctant to rethink things and perhaps make a change or two. Even if a design modification is conceptually simple, the modification may require a flowchart box and line insertion that will force a complete redrawing just to get the chart to fit nicely on one page. When used for program documentation, what happens to flowcharts after a program modification? Even if someone else is assigned to update the program flowcharts, he or she may try to save time by squeezing the modifications in on the existing charts, perhaps in a different color ink. After a few years and many modifications, one may have an interesting, modernistic work of art but a very poor flowchart. If a flowchart generator program is available, this effect can admittedly be avoided; however, the results of flowchart generators are usually no more helpful than the original code.

In summary, programmers and managers should really think twice before using time and resources for constructing program flowcharts, whether it be for program design or documentation. For good program design, we recommend the top-down approach, which is discussed in Chapter 3.

GLOBAL VARIABLES, FUNCTIONS, AND SUBROUTINES

Global Variables

The use of variables to represent updated entities is familiar to all programmers. Guidelines for the effective use of variables are seldom discussed. Nevertheless, this topic is of paramount importance in writing quality programs.

Consider a "block" (i.e., a sequence of statements) of code, B, that performs some computation, f, on two variables, X1 and X2, to yield a result, Y, as illustrated in Fig. 5.5. In any such block there may, of course, be other intermediate variables needed for the computation. Assume for the moment that each of the intermediate variables is not used outside the block of code B except for one variable, V. In order to abstract the computation f in B, one must then not only consider the computation of Y from X1 and X2, but also consider the effect on V. In this case, we say that V is "active in" or "global to" the block.

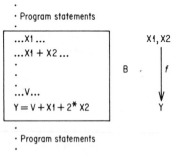

Fig. 5.5   A "block" of code

The use of multiple global variables is a frequent cause of undue complexity in computer programs. To abstract the computation of a logical block of code, the changes applied to global variables must be considered.

There are several critical problems associated with the use of multiple

Example 5.1 Functions Vs. Subroutines

```
        EXAMPLE 5.1A  A SIMPLE FUNCTION

100         DEF FNA(R)
110 REM
120 REM     **  FUNCTION TO COMPUTE THE AREA OF A CIRCLE
130         DATA 3.14159
140             READ P
150             LET FNA = P * (R**2)
160         FNEND



        EXAMPLE 5.1B  A SIMPLE SUBROUTINE

100 REM     **  SUBROUTINE TO COMPUTE THE AREA OF A CIRCLE
110         DATA 3.14159
120             READ P
130             LET A = P * (R**2)
140         RETURN
```

---

global variables. First, the complexity of a block of statements rapidly increases with even a small increase in the number of variables. Second, if the number of statements over which the variables range is large, then the intent of referencing statements can be difficult to comprehend. Importantly, any change to a program outside the block of statements can affect the correctness of the block itself.

BASIC does not have a formal block-structure feature; indeed, all variables in BASIC are global and the problems mentioned above can become disastrous when one writes large programs. We feel strongly, however, that the power of BASIC would be greatly enhanced if it were designed so as to limit the visibility of variables.

BASIC is careful to make the following (commonly held) distinction. A "function" refers to a subprogram that returns a value. A "subroutine" refers to a subprogram that produces a change in a variable outside the subprogram. In particular, consider the simple declarations of Example 5.1. In Example 5.1a, the subprogram to compute area, FNA, is used as a function. For example, if the value of R (radius) is 3.0, an evaluation of the expression

$$1.0 + FNA(R)$$

yields one, plus the value of the function. In Example 5.2b, a subroutine is used. For example, if the value of A (area) is 3.0, the statement

$$GOSUB\ 100$$

results in assigning to A the value computed by the subroutines. The difference between functions and subroutines is important but not always obvious. Generally speaking, functions are used in place of *expressions* to return *values,* whereas subroutines are used in place of *statements* to perform *assignments* to external variables. It is possible in BASIC to write subprograms that both return a value and cause an effect outside the subprogram. As a rule, it is unwise to do this as we shall see in subsequent examples.

Functions

Loosely speaking, the *context* of a function is its relation to other sections of a program. If a function alters a quantity global to itself, then it exhibits a *context effect*. Basically, a function can produce a context effect in two ways: by altering its arguments or by altering a global variable.

**Example 5.2 Context Effect Accompanying the Returned Value
of a Function**

```
                    EXAMPLE 5.2A   ONE PROGRAM

       100            LET A = 10
       110            LET B = 3
       120            LET C = FNF(B) + FNF(B)
       130            PRINT C
       140         END
       150 REM
       160 REM
       170         DEF FNF (X)
       180            LET A   = A + 1
       190            LET FNF = A * X
       200         FNEND



                    EXAMPLE 5.2B   AN EQUIVALENT PROGRAM?

       100            LET A = 10
       110            LET B = 3
       120            LET C = 2 * FNF(B)
       130            PRINT C
       140         END
       150 REM
       160 REM
       170         DEF FNF (X)
       180            LET A   = A + 1
       190            LET FNF = A * X
       200         FNEND
```

Programmers who write functions with context effects can get unpleasant surprises. Consider Example 5.2. These two program segments are identical except for the replacement of the expression

$$FNF(B) + FNF(B)$$

in Example 5.2a by the expression

$$2.0*FNF(B)$$

in Example 5.2b. These two programs are not equivalent because

Example 5.3 Context Effect Accompanying the Assignment
to a Global Variable in Common

```
                     EXAMPLE 5.3A   ONE PROGRAM

100              LET A = 10
110              LET B = 3
120              LET C = FNF(B) + FNG(B)
130              PRINT C
140          END
150 REM
160 REM
170              DEF FNF (X)
180                  LET A   = A + 1
190                  LET FNF = A * X
200              FNEND
210 REM
220 REM
230              DEF FNG (X)
240                  LET A   = A + 2
250                  LET FNG = A * X
260              FNEND



                     EXAMPLE 5.3B   AN EQUIVALENT PROGRAM?

100              LET A = 10
110              LET B = 3
120              LET C = FNG(B) + FNF(B)
130              PRINT C
140          END
150 REM
160 REM
170              DEF FNF (X)
180                  LET A   = A + 1
190                  LET FNF = A * X
200              FNEND
210 REM
220 REM
230              DEF FNG (X)
240                  LET A   = A + 2
250                  LET FNG = A * X
260              FNEND
```

$$FNF(B) + FNF(B) = (11.0)*(3.0) + (12.0)*(3.0)$$
$$= 69.0$$
$$2.0*FNF(B) \quad\quad = (2.0)*(11.0)*(3.0)$$
$$= 66.0$$

Hence we lose a fundamental property of addition. The problem is caused by the context effect in the function FNF with the assignment of $(A + 1.0)$ to A, where A is global to the function.

Strictly speaking, Example 5.2a is invalid in some implementations, since identical calls in a single statement to the function FNF yield different results. Interestingly, some processors sidestep this error by evaluation of FNF(B) only once; in these implementations, we do not lose the fundamental property of addition, but the context effect is obscured.

A similar case arises in Example 5.3. Again these examples are identical except that

$$FNF(B) + FNG(B)$$

in 5.3a is replaced by

$$FNG(B) + FNF(B)$$

in 5.3b. Using a left-to-right evaluation, the written values for C, 72 and 75, are not the same. Here, the familiar commutative property of addition is lost because of the assignment to a global variable. Certainly many programmers would be surprised to learn that FNF(B) + FNG(B) is not equivalent in this case to FNG(B) + FNF(B). Since BASIC employs conventional mathematical notation, it is dangerous to write functions that violate the properties of established mathematical systems.

The case against context effects becomes even more severe when we need to change a program. Change is a daily occurrence in programming. Someone may find a more efficient algorithm, more output may be needed, a bug may be detected, or revised specifications may be given. If a piece of code to be changed has context effects, then those effects must be accounted for. The resulting changes may imply the need to delve deeply into the entire program for a clear understanding of what effects a function or subroutine has on other parts of the program. Adding a few extra lines of code for that desirable change may kill the correctness of another piece of code. As a result, another change may be needed to right matters, and so on. Even if this process succeeds, it is not likely to add to the clarity or flexibility of the program. Had the original program been written without context effects, the function could be changed *without* looking at the rest of the program.

Next consider Example 5.4, a case in which a function subprogram alters the value of an argument. The problem here is that two function calls with the same arguments return *different* values. In larger programs, such a use of arguments is quite dangerous. In making a correction or alteration, the programmer may unwittingly alter the value of subsequent calls to the function. Furthermore, to replace FNF with another procedure, the programmer must consider the main program in order to ensure the proper handling of global variables.

Example 5.4 Context Effect on the Arguments of a Function

```
100          LET A = 4
110          LET B = FNF(5, A)
120          LET C = FNF(5, A)
130          PRINT B, C
140    END
150 REM
160 REM
170          DEF FNF (X, Y)
180          LET Y   = Y + X
190          LET FNF = X * Y
200    FNEND
```

An interesting problem arises in some implementations that do not check whether an argument, which may be a constant, is redefined by a call to a subprogram. Consider Example 5.4 again, where the main program reads as follows:

$$\text{LET B} = \text{FNF}(5.0, 4.0)$$
$$\text{LET C} = \text{FNF}(5.0, 4.0)$$
$$\text{PRINT B,C}$$

If the stored value of 4.0 is updated to 9.0, we have a nonconstant constant!

In short, functions with context effects are to be avoided, unless there is a compelling reason to use them.

Subroutines

The purpose of a subroutine is to produce some effect external to itself, not to return a value. Essentially, a subroutine consists of a group of statements isolated from a main routine or program for convenience or clarity. The problems encountered with context effects in subroutines are quite similar to those encountered in functions. There is one important exception. Since a subroutine is designed to update a specific set of variables, each of the changed variables should be included in the list of arguments. Consider Example 5.5. By using all assigned variables in the argument list in each subroutine call, the reader can speed up

**Example 5.5 Context Effect in Subroutines by Assignment
to a Global Variable**

```
                        EXAMPLE 5.5A   POOR


        100             LET A = 17
        110             LET B = 3
        120             LET X = A
        130 REM
        140             GOSUB 190
        150             PRINT A, B
        160     END
        170 REM
        180 REM
        190             LET X = 2 *  (X+1)
        200             LET B = 5 *  X
        210     RETURN




                        EXAMPLE 5.5B   BETTER


        100             LET A = 17
        110             LET B = 3
        120             LET X = A
        130             LET Y = B
        140 REM
        150             GOSUB 230
        160             LET A = X
        170             LET B = Y
        180             PRINT A, B
        190 REM
        200     END
        210 REM
        220 REM
        230             LET X = 2 *  (X+1)
        240             LET Y = 5 *  X
        250     RETURN
```

tracing the changed variables, since he will not have to look through the body of the subroutine.

Exceptions to the Rules and Summary

There are, of course, cases where global variables and context effects may indeed be useful. For example, there may be names and arrays whose (often used) values remain constant within the program. Making these quantities global to the entire program certainly causes no problems. The global use of the names P1 (Player 1), P2 (Player 2), and V (Vacant) in the Kriegspiel program illustrates this point.

More importantly, there may be variables and arrays whose values do change but are used in so many procedures that passing them as arguments in every call would result in a lengthy or inefficient code. The global use of the array to represent the current board status in the Kriegspiel program illustrates this point. In such cases, it may be justifiable to make the quantities global to all procedures.

Nevertheless, global variables and context effects can cause serious problems. If they are used, they should be used sparingly. In summary, we give the following rules of thumb:

1. *Functions*

   Use a function only for its returned value.

   Do not use a function when you need a subroutine.

   Do not alter formal parameters.

   Do not alter global variables.

   Use unique variable names within the subprogram body.

2. *Subroutines*

   Do not use a subroutine when you need a function.

   Do not alter global variables.

   Use unique variable names within the subprogram body.

RECURSION

Loosely speaking, recursion is a method of definition in which the object being defined is used within the definition. For example, consider the following definition of the word "descendant":

> *A descendant of a person is a son or daughter of the person, or a descendant of a son or daughter.*

In this definition *all* the descendants of the person are simply and precisely accounted for. A nonrecursive definition of "descendant" that takes all possibilities into consideration would be the following:

A descendant of a person is a son or daughter of the person, or a grandson or granddaughter of the person, or a great-grandson or great-granddaughter of the person, etc.

In this case, the definition is lengthier and less succinct than the recursive definition. It is interesting to note how dictionaries attempt to skirt recursion in the definition of "descendant." "Descendant" is often defined in terms of "ancestor," whereas "ancestor" is defined in terms of "descendant." The two definitions are, in fact, mutually recursive.

In programming, recursive definitions apply to function and subroutine declarations. A recursive subprogram declaration is one that has the potential to invoke itself. In other words, it is defined partially in terms of itself.

It seems unfortunate that recursion is not available in standard BASIC. There are many problems for which a recursive solution would be the natural vehicle. In mathematics, recursive definitions abound. Yet only a very few implementations offer a recursive capability. Even then, it is limited and often inefficient. Thus a BASIC programmer must develop the ability to write any program nonrecursively, that is, using iterative rather than recursive schemes.

The primary point of this section is that in many instances recursive definitions are clearer, more succinct, or more natural, than their nonrecursive counterparts, even if they are less efficient. Recursive definitions often follow naturally using the top-down programming approach. A clear idea of the nature and power of recursive definitions can be a valuable aid to a BASIC programmer. Even if recursion is not available, we feel that the concept is so important that we cannot resist including a section on this topic. For the following examples, let us assume a BASIC recursive capability.

Suppose we wish to sum the elements of an integer array. Simple arithmetic gives us the following equality:

$$\sum_{i=1}^{n} a_i = a_1 \qquad \text{if } n = 1$$

$$\sum_{i=1}^{n} a_i = a_n + \sum_{i=1}^{n-1} a_i \qquad \text{if } n \geq 2$$

Stated in English, the sum of the elements of an array is the last element plus the sum of the first $n - 1$ elements. If the array has only one element, the sum is the single element. With these facts in mind, it is possible to write the function FNS recursively, as in Example 5.6a. Its nonrecursive counterpart is given in Example 5.6b.

To ensure that the recursive definition of FNS is understood, observe the following analysis of the function subprogram when applied to a four-element array containing the numbers 3, 6, 8, and 2.

Depth of Recursive Calls	*Value of FNS*
1	FNS(A,4)
2	2 + FNS(A,3)
3	2 + (8 + FNS(A,2))
4	2 + (8 + (6 + FNS(A,1)))
4	2 + (8 + (6 + 3))
3	2 + (8 + 9)
2	2 + 17
1	19

**Example 5.6 Sum of the Elements in an Array Defined with
and without Recursion**

```
          EXAMPLE 5.6A   RECURSIVE DEFINITION


100        DEF FNS (A, N)
110 REM
120        DIM A(N)
130 REM
140            IF (N <> 1) GOTO 170
150                LET FNS = A(1)
160                GOTO 200
170                LET FNS = A(N) + FNS (A, N-1)
180 REM
190 REM
200        FNEND
210        END




          EXAMPLE 5.6B   NON-RECURSIVE DEFINITION


100        DEF FNS (A, N)
110 REM
120        DIM A(N)
130 REM
140            LET FNS = 0
150            FOR I = 1 TO N
160                LET FNS = FNS + A(I)
170            NEXT I
180 REM
190 REM
200        FNEND
210        END
```

An example particularly well suited to recursive definition is the implementation of Euclid's algorithm for computing the greatest common divisor of two positive integers, M and N. The FNG function subprogram requires an additional integer function FNR(I,J) that returns the remainder when I is divided by J.

The definitions are shown in Example 5.7. For comparison, a nonrecursive definition for the same function subprogram is also given. The nonrecursive definitions are slightly larger and less clear. The properties of the algorithm are still present, but they are hidden by the looping constructs.

Example 5.7 Euclid's Greatest Common Divisor Algorithm
Defined with and without Recursion

```
                EXAMPLE 5.7A  RECURSIVE DEFINITION


100         DEF FNG (F, S)
110 REM
120             IF (F >= S)  GOTO 160
130                 LET FNG = FNG (S, F)
140             GOTO 230
150 REM
160                 LET R = FNR (F, S)
170                 IF (R <> 0)  GOTO 170
180                     LET FNG = S
190                 GOTO 230
200 REM
210                     LET FNG = FNG (F, S)
220 REM
230             FNEND




                EXAMPLE 5.7B  NON-RECURSIVE DEFINITION


100         DEF FNG (F, S)
110 REM
120             IF (F >= S)  GOTO 170
130                 LET L = F
140                 LET H = S
150             GOTO 200
160 REM
170                 LET L = S
180                 LET H = F
190 REM
200             LET R = FNR (H, L)
210             IF (R = 0)  GOTO 250
220                 LET L = R
230             GOTO 200
240 REM
250                 LET FNG = L
260 REM
270             FNEND
```

Merely knowing what recursion looks like is not enough. It is also necessary to know (1) if recursion is applicable to the problem at hand, and (2) how to
apply it. There are no formal rules in either case, although some guidelines. One
is that the notion of mathematical "induction" is a close analog to recursion.
Induction is a method of definition in which (1) initial values of a function are
defined explicitly (the base step), and (2) other values are implicitly defined in
terms of previous values (the inductive step). If the definition given in the second
step applies to all elements other than the initial values, then the principle of
mathematical induction asserts that the function is (explicitly) well-defined for all
values in its domain.

To illustrate the method of inductive definition, consider the sequence of
Fibonacci numbers. The first two numbers are both 1, and each successive
number in the sequence is the sum of the two preceding numbers. More
explicitly,

N = 1   BASE STEP   FNF(1) = 1
N = 2   FNF(2) = 1

N ≥ 3   INDUCTIVE STEP   FNF(N) = FNF(N−1) + FNF(N−2)

The step from this inductive definition to a recursive function declaration is small. A function subprogram to generate the Nth Fibonacci number is shown defined recursively and nonrecursively in Example 5.8. The Fibonacci function written recursively parrots the inductive definition and clearly shows the main property of the Fibonacci numbers. While the nonrecursive example uses the same property, it is harder to detect. The additional code required to write the function nonrecursively is mostly bookkeeping. Also note that in the recursive definition, the function subprogram FNF is recursively invoked twice. Without a good optimizing compiler, this double invocation is quite inefficient.

A great deal could be said about recursion, and a good deal of the literature is devoted to the subject. For our purposes, the point is simple. Understand the use of recursion and the translation from a recursive definition to a nonrecursive BASIC code. You may find that recursion is a valuable addition to your programming skills.

**Example 5.8 The Fibonacci Sequence Defined with
and without Recursion**

```
               EXAMPLE 5.8A   RECURSIVE DEFINITION


     100       DEF FNF (N)
     110 REM
     120           IF (N > 2)  GOTO 160
     130               LET FNF = 1
     140               GOTO 180
     150 REM
     160               LET FNF = FNF (N-1) + FNF (N-2)
     170 REM
     180           FNEND




               EXAMPLE 5.8B   NONRECURSIVE DEFINITION


     100       DEF FNF (N)
     110 REM
     120           IF (N > 2)  GOTO 160
     130               LET FNF = 1
     140               GOTO 240
     150 REM
     160               LET F1 = 1
     170               LET F2 = 1
     180               FOR I = 3 TO N
     190                   LET FNF = F1 + F2
     200                   LET F1  = F2
     210                   LET F2  = FNF
     220               NEXT I
     230 REM
     240           FNEND
```

VERY LARGE PROGRAMS

This book has focused on a single topic: the writing of quality programs by the individual programmer. The development of large software systems obviously involves other issues far beyond the scope of this book. But because of the importance of large systems, we introduce some of the quality issues here. Our ideas are based mainly on the work of Cave [Ref. C1].

Premises

We begin with a number of premises that we believe are vital for the success of any large programming project.

1. The development of user-oriented software systems is first and foremost a management problem.

This is a difficult premise to accept because poor management reflects right to the top of any organization. Nevertheless, this premise is vital since project failures are generally the result of improper or inexperienced management and not a lack of technical ability. The management responsibility requires not only knowledge, experience, and judgment, but also a high level of perspective. To avoid major mistakes in policy, it is vital to have a good perspective of

a. The experience, skills, and tools required to complete a given task
b. The availability of these resources within the organization
c. The importance of establishing the credibility of outside experts through reliable references
d. The need for constant vigilance against the dangers of sacrificing effectiveness for program efficiency.

2. The success of any software system is always finally measured by the ultimate user.

In order for capable managers to succeed, they must have an environment that responds quickly and is easily controlled. The willingness on the part of prospective users to order and pay for services rendered on a continuing basis is the essential element for effective control. When "dollar control" flows directly from the end user down through the ranks of the developer, it creates an environment less prone to politics, cleverness, and internal disagreements.

Measuring management ability largely by user satisfaction also creates a willingness on the part of management to call on outside expertise and forces attention on the need for accurate performance measurement.

This environment concept closely relates to Baker's work [Ref. B1]. The chief programmer team is organized around a chief with exceptional experience and control. One gets the feeling that this chief has one finger on the pulse of the entire project, while the tips of the other fingers control all members of the team.

Within certain organizations, only a strong technical ability backed by strong personal credibility can create the environment needed to provide control and to obtain response from a team of programmers. The chief programmer team approach thus appears suitable for creating the management control essential to success in most organizations.

3. *The overall project management must not be divorced from software development.*

Independent of the individual system characteristics, and a highly technical environment notwithstanding, overall project management must be directly responsible for developing the software.

First, it is all too easy to blame software failures on any organizational unit other than the one under question. Identifying the project management with the technical problems ensures that management is indeed responsible for the entire effort.

Second, over and above the development of programs, the very nature of software development implies the need to develop the organization and managing procedures to be used in final operational systems. This decision-making process is implicitly given to the software developer. The reason, which is not readily apparent, is that the very nature of software development implicitly places the responsibility for designing a usable system upon those doing the creating, and not upon the user.

4. *Software development must be a sequence of clearly isolated phases.*

Changes *will* occur in project emphasis, personnel, time frames, user requirements, and the development environment. This implies that it is necessary to:

   a. Allow time for the developer to gain experience and to discover the peculiarities of a given application.
   b. Allow time to expose the user's personnel to relevant techniques.
   c. Allow for well-controlled changes in user requirements
   d. Allow for reviews and GO-NOGO decisions after each design phase.

Only by a breakdown of the development effort into well-defined and clearly separate units can the problems of change be met.

5. *An integrated set of standards must form the foundation for controlling the entire software development effort.*

To acquire and maintain control, management must have the tools to impose a strict discipline at the very beginning. Strict standards are the key to this discipline. Typical standards include the following:

   a. *Project Definition.* These standards specify the form for stating the objectives, constraints, and overall project plan.
   b. *System Specification.* These standards focus on complete specifications of system characteristics.

c. *Documentation*. These standards must focus on complete specifications of system characteristics. The standards should ensure that all documents are self-contained and easily read.

d. *Programming*. Generally these standards cover style, structure, and internal documentation of programs. Strict rules on the use of procedures, spacing and indentation, control structures, and choice of variable names are especially important. The ideal place to enforce these standards is the language compiler. Barring that, program reading by managers and programmers is a good alternative.

e. *Testing and Quality Control*. Prior to coding, standard procedures must be established on developing test data and the buildup to a full cycle test. Good procedures for system modification and maintenance of the external documentation set must also be established prior to coding.

The Incremental Approach

We next outline an approach to the building of large systems that is based on the above premises. This approach, called the "Incremental Method," is due to Cave [Ref. C1]. It is incremental in the following senses:

a. It dictates a multiphase (not a single-phase) design effort.
b. Resources are committed on an incremental basis.
c. There are a series of clearly delineated review points.

Each phase follows a highly structured pattern of plan, do, write, and review.

Phase 1: Development of Project Objectives

The first phase is an explicit study of user objectives by the project management. Frequent contacts must be made with the user to develop a clear understanding of user problems. Emphasis must be placed on extracting relevant problem concerns and the elimination of arbitrary constraints that can only hamper further development. Hardware and software constraints must also be resolved. The result of this phase is a written description of user objectives. At this phase, it may not be possible to estimate the entire system development costs. At the very least, a careful estimate must be made to determine the cost of the next phase.

Finally, both the user and developer must allow ample time to review the proposed objectives. If further development effort is justified, then the next phase can be executed.

Phase 2: Functional Specification

This phase focuses on a detailed analysis of user requirements. The result of this phase is a set of documents that functionally defines the entire system as seen by the user. We believe that this definition should be so complete that the specifications will ultimately serve as a basis for the user documentation.

In sharp contrast with many conventional system development procedures, this phase is precisely the time to prepare user manuals. It is unwise to proceed further without giving the ultimate user a detailed idea of what to expect from the proposed system. It is certainly easier to change an unsatisfactory design during this phase, rather than after coding.

Finally, a complete review must be undertaken to decide if the detailed specification is still acceptable to the user and still feasible from the viewpoint of the system designer.

Phase 3: Environmental Specification

This phase is a period for determining environment requirements, such as equipment configurations, languages, and support software.

The first consideration should be a review of the existing technology. Trade-offs to meet the functional specification must be resolved. Any severe constraints on the hardware, support software, or operating system must be recognized. If the existing operating system or hardware requires major changes, then the cost of necessary changes must be defined.

The second concern should be the resolution of critical problems for which research or development is needed. Typical of such problems would be the development of unusual operating system algorithms or the design of a critical data structure for information storage and retrieval. Failure to resolve these problems early may undermine the success of the entire proposed system independently of the overall design approach.

Finally, a careful review should be undertaken to assess all required technical support. Any detected deficiencies in the hardware, operating system, or software support must be accounted for. Costs in time, people, and money should be estimated. Again, a GO-NOGO decision must be made by user and designer in concert.

Phase 4: System Design

This phase is devoted to detailed program documentation of the entire system and a matching of the design with effective personnel. The required programming personnel must first be given responsibility for documenting (before coding!) any proposed code. The procedures for doing this lie in the hands of the technical management. Each required document must be acceptable to management with full regard to the detailed functional specification standards.

It is important to stress the integration of individual involvement with the overall system documentation. Strict quality control must be placed on the system documentation from this point on. Poor individual documentation will be a likely predictor of poor code, and any such low-quality performance must be detected early. Any functional changes resulting from this phase must be incorporated in the design specifications themselves.

Finally again, the review. A review at this point is critical, for significant software costs will be involved if progress to the next phase is agreed upon.

Phase 5: System Construction

This phase is primarily concerned with writing and testing the programs for the system. Because of the rather elaborate preparation of the previous phases, this phase should proceed more smoothly and accurately than would generally be expected. The first major concern is the adoption of strict programming standards. The standards should include the choice of a high-level language, programming techniques, restrictions on program spacing and indentation, control structures, and the organization of programming teams.

The second major concern is a strict scheduling of program assignments and the required hardware facilities. It is all too easy to accumulate day-by-day slippage due to improper coordination of program writing and hardware test facilities.

Formal modification procedures must be developed to process corrections, refinements, or user requests for changes. Continuous maintenance and "shakedown" of all the programming documentation is vital to the integrity of the whole design effort. Loss of control over this activity can only lead to a slow but steady erosion of product quality.

Finally, management and the user must make a GO-NOGO decision to field the system. If agreement is reached, that is the next phase.

Phase 6: Real Environment Testing

During this period, the entire system is subjected to full-scale use under a simulated real user environment. The objective is the development of a full-cycle test whose effectiveness is satisfactory to both user and developer.

Representative user personnel are trained to use the system and to shake down the user's documentation. Formal modification procedures must be developed to process requests for corrections, refinements, and enhancements.

As the testing nears completion, detailed plans for the next phase, live operation, must be prepared. It is all too easy to let this planning fall by the wayside, but ultimately the user will have to live with the system. Planning should at least include cost estimates for steady state operation, and recovery procedures in case of system failure.

Finally, the user and developer must make the final GO-NOGO decision on whether to put the system into live operation or to return to make changes.

Phase 7: Live Operation

If the preceding phases have been properly completed, live operation will be easily effected.

Formal procedures to determine responsibility for possible system errors and the corresponding correction process must be developed. The system maintenance agent as well as the user should be able to initiate correction requests. Formal procedures for processing requests for system refinements and enhancements must also be developed. If there are multiple systems in the field, these procedures must preserve the system identity and the integrity of the documentation. To reduce total documentation and program modification efforts, it may be desirable to accumulate modification requests as long as the system remains operable.

Last, the user and developer should periodically review the entire effort. The level and formality of reviews will, of course, vary. In any event, formal user/designer reviews should take place annually at a minimum.

Conclusions

There are no simple techniques for developing large programs of high quality. What we do maintain, however, is that there are viable management guidelines for acquiring and maintaining project control. These guidelines can be backed up by a clean breakdown of projects into distinct phases and a set of strict standards.

One important point must be noted. The crucial parameter for measuring project success is user satisfaction. However, when overall user requirements cause estimates of time, people, or funding to exceed imposed constraints, it is necessary that a decision be made to either relax the requirements or halt the project! The decision to continue a project under uncertain estimates of required costs definitely places the responsibility for possible excess on management's shoulders. It is, therefore, essential that any method for management control must allow for periodic continuation decisions so that halts can ensure a minimum waste of resources.

One of the initial difficulties of the approach given here is the notion of "front-end loading," or the rather large involvement with the early noncoding stages of a project. This concept is initially hard to accept. Especially under an incremental funding arrangement, it appears that the user is paying a high price in the beginning and getting little return. However, when the detailed documentation is completed (the end of the functional specification phase), users are generally enthusiastic about the approach.

SOME PARTING COMMENTS

We would like to close this final chapter with a variety of thoughts on the notion of software quality. These thoughts have been partially expressed in previous chapters. They are neither new nor rigorously supported, but they do sum up a number of important issues.

Programmers are faced with numerous difficult problems. One point often confused is the difference between problem solving and programming. "Problem solving" can be viewed as the act of developing an algorithm to solve a given problem, "programming" as the act of transforming an algorithm into the linguistic concepts of a given programming language. In its conception, this book is primarily about programming, not problem solving. The techniques discussed in it will not necessarily help the programmer find a more efficient method of sorting, a faster method for computing Fourier Transforms, or a better heuristic for a chess-playing program.

The programmer's task is usually an intricate combination of both problem solving and programming. The issues in problem solving are vital to writing effective computer programs. Yet it is now well recognized that the "programming" of a given algorithm is far from trivial, and that the programmer should use all the available techniques of programming to ensure that his devised algorithm is clear. While good programming techniques will offer strong guidelines for the development of a good solution to a problem, we must admit that "programming," as conceived here, is only part of the programmer's task.

A somewhat controversial issue treated in this work is that of controlling GOTO statements. The case against the GOTO is primarily due to the concentration that it entails on the flow of control rather than on the basic computations, functions, and procedures needed to solve a given problem. Although we strongly believe it would be wise to recommend that future languages provide alternatives to the GOTO, in current languages the GOTO does exist, and in standard BASIC it is indeed impossible to avoid.

The real issue for the programmer is how to manage the complexity of his program. The indiscriminate use of the GOTO is clearly to be avoided, for its abuse can easily make a given algorithm opaque. Yet when wisely used, the GOTO can be just as transparent as alternative control structures. Our final recommendation: Use the GOTO, but use it wisely.

As mentioned in this chapter, the use of program flowcharts has been avoided in this text. As a method of program design, program flowcharts have been highly overvalued. The top-down approach to programming suppresses the use of these flowcharts in favor of highlighting a functional or procedural approach to program design. The case against program flowcharts is similar to the case against the GOTO. The lines and arrows can easily lead the user into a highly sequential mode of thinking. Furthermore, there is a tendency to think that once a program flowchart has been designed, the programming process is just about complete. Unfortunately, this is seldom the case. The programmer would be well-advised to try another approach whenever he or she thinks a program flowchart is needed.

Consider the Kriegspiel program of Chapter 3. In this program no complete module requires a listing of more than two pages of text, and most modules fit on a single page. This characteristic results from human engineering. We all know how difficult it can be to follow a long program. In any lengthy program, we usually try to abstract a logical portion of it that will give us an indication of its overall computation. Every programmer should recognize this fact and write each program so that each logical unit is clearly isolated on a page or two.

One underestimated problem in programming is that of keeping to language standards. Admittedly, our languages are so diffuse in scope and often so lacking in transparent linguistic features that it is hard not to introduce or use features that make up for some of the shortcomings. For example, the lack of better looping structures deserves remedy. Yet if we are to insist that programs are to be portable or that users can understand the programs written in other implementations, then we must stick to language features that are common to most (if not all) implementations. Even in writing a book such as this, the problem of keeping to a "standard" was difficult. Despite the difficulty, two points are worth mentioning. We should encourage the development of *more* and *better* standard definitions, and unless there is a compelling reason to do otherwise, we should adhere to the standards we have.

One difficulty, not often felt by programmers using PL/I, PASCAL, or several other languages, is the often defeating cycle of arguments promulgating the use of BASIC. The cycle goes something like this. We want to teach prospective programmers a language that will be of practical value. While other languages may be more useful or powerful, BASIC is by far the most simple. Therefore, we should stick to BASIC.

This cycle in part sums up the circumstances for the wide use of BASIC. Yet, if we view the computer-based professions as about 30 years old, BASIC, as originally conceived, is now fairly old—about half the lifespan of modern computer science. BASIC clearly lacks a good facility for manipulating strings, a facility for grouping compound statements, alphabetic statement labels, a generous facility for data structures, and numerous, now well-accepted language features. Have we learned so little in recent years that we cannot break this cycle? We hope not.

As regards the standard definition of BASIC, there is one issue that, above all else, we violently disagree with. It is the limitation of names to at most one character. To us there is no question that limiting names to one character poses an enormous problem in writing clear programs. At almost every juncture in this book, we have had severely difficult problems in developing names that were compatible with standard BASIC. Furthermore, a "break" character would be useful to interpret long names. How nice it would be to use names like "X-COORDINATE," "NEXT-SQUARE," or "NUM-VALUES-READ." Trying to shorten such names to one character is a time-consuming and unrewarding task. We strongly urge that future versions of BASIC allow the longer names to be punctuated by an appropriate break character.

Further, it seems quite reasonable to us to allow for a simple BLOCK-IF sequence. The structure could be implemented easily by restricting programmers to one level of nesting. This feature has been added to FORTRAN 77 with the effect that even a long program such as Kriegspiel was implemented virtually GOTO-lessly!

We would also like to stress the need for proper functions and subroutines. If a distinction were made between global and local reference, parameters could be used easily and side effects could be eliminated.

There are many other issues that need to be investigated. Among these are the need for better documentation of programs, better programming languages, the establishment of problem definition techniques, the development of a more manageable successor to BASIC, and the promotion of human factors.

The final issue is the critical need to upgrade the entire programming effort.

With all of the new interest in programming, progress is certainly on its way. We must discipline ourselves to this interest but only adopt what is really progressive. Perhaps the best motivation is to remember that the program you write today may be the program you will have to change next year.

EXERCISES

Exercise 5.1   (Global Variables in Functions)
What is printed by the following piece of code?

```
100          LET A = 1
110          LET A = FNF(FNF(2)) + A
120          PRINT A
130     END
140 REM
150 REM
160 REM
170          DEF FNF (X)
180             LET A   = X + FNG (X)
190             LET FNF = 2 * A
200          FNEND
210 REM
220 REM
230 REM
240          DEF FNG (X)
250             LET A   = 2 * (X + 1)
260             LET FNG = A
270          FNEND
```

Exercise 5.2

It is likely that you disagree strongly with at least one of the topics discussed in this chapter. Pick the one that you disagree with the most and prepare a comprehensive counterproposal. After the customary number of rewrites, have someone else read it. (Hint: Choose a friend to do the reading.) When you are finished, send the results to the authors.

Exercise 5.3

This exercise is for those who have just completed reading our brief text. First, we want to thank you for the compliment of reading this book. Second, compare the style of the next program you write with one you wrote prior to reading our book. Evaluate the impact of our book on your programming style and send us a letter.

Exercise 5.4

Below are two advanced topics that we would have liked to discuss in this chapter. Pick the one that interests you the most, discuss the relevant issues, seek out the opinions of others, and present proposals which resolve some of the problems therein. Submit your results to a conference:

Topic 1: "The Problem with Problem Definition"

Issues: How should one detail inputs and outputs? What is a "functional" specification? What constitutes a "complete" definition? How much of a definition can be used for documentation? Where do implementation requirements go? What about condition-action lists versus decision tables? How should the layout and organization of a good, complete definition appear?

Topic 2: "The Global Variable Problem"

Issues: Should functions or subroutines be declared within main programs? What changes would you make in BASIC to encourage better isolation of modules.

Exercise 5.5

There once was a frog named Mr. Croak who was beset with three daughters of marriageable age, Ribbit1, Ribbit2, and Ribbit3. Now the only eligible male frog, Horatio, fell for Ribbit2 and proceeded to ask for her leg in marriage. However, Mr. Croak, concerned with the marriage prospects for Ribbit1 and Ribbit3, proposed the following: Whichever one of his daughters leaped the farthest would become Horatio's wife. Now, Horatio knew, but Mr. Croak didn't, that Ribbit1 could jump three lily pads, that Ribbit2 could jump twice as far as Ribbit1, and that Ribbit3 could jump only one third as far as Ribbit2. Thus Horatio readily agreed and persuaded Mr. Croak that the following computer program should determine who would wed him. (Note: R1, R2, and R3 denote the lengths of the jumps of Ribbits 1, 2, and 3.)

```
100            LET R1 = 3
110            LET R2 = FNF (R1)
120            LET R3 = FNG (R2)
130            PRINT 'RIBBIT1 = '; R1, ' RIBBIT2 = '; R2, ' RIBBIT3 = '; R3
140       END
150 REM
160 REM
170 REM
180       DEF FNF (X)
190            LET X   = 2 * X
200            LET FNF = X
210       FNEND
220 REM
230 REM
240 REM
250       DEF FNG (X)
260            LET X   = (1 / 3) * X
270            LET FNG = X
280       FNEND
```

What is the moral of the story?

Exercise 5.6

Take the rest of the afternoon off. (We knew we could use this somewhere.)

APPENDIX A

Summary of Program Structures

General Requirements

[GEN-1]   Any violation of the program standards must be approved by someone appointed to enforce the standards.

[GEN-2]   Each installation shall have established alignment (prettyprinting) conventions.

[GEN-3]   No program unit may exceed two pages of code.

[GEN-4]   All programs shall include the following comment:

REM	**	PROGRAM TITLE	Brief title
REM	**		
REM	**	WRITTEN BY	Name of author(s)
REM	**	DATE WRITTEN	Date of first execution
REM	**	WRITTEN FOR	Responsible unit
REM	**		
REM	**	PROGRAM INTENT	Brief program summary
		.	
		.	
		.	
REM	**	INPUT FILES	
REM	**	file-name	Brief description of use
		.	
		.	
		.	
REM	**	OUTPUT FILES	
REM	**	file-name	Brief description of use
		.	

Data Statements

[DATA-1]   DATA statements which are used to initialize constants must appear before the first executable statement.

[DATA-2]   DATA statements which are used to initialize non-file oriented input variables must appear after the END statement.

[DATA-3]   All numeric values, character strings, and arrays that remain constant throughout a program must be given a name and a value in a DATA statement.

[DATA-4]   No variable (i.e., one whose value is changed in an executable statement) may be initialized in a DATA statement.

Control Structures

[CNTRL-1]   GOTO statements may only be used in the following forms:

      (a) ℓ_1 IF (logical-expression) GOTO ℓ_2
                 statement-sequence$_1$
                 GOTO ℓ_1
         ℓ_2 statement-sequence$_2$

      (b) ℓ_1 statement-sequence$_1$
                 IF (logical-expression) GOTO ℓ_2
                 statement-sequence$_2$
                 GOTO ℓ_2
         ℓ_2 statement-sequence$_3$

      (c)   IF (logical-expresssion) GOTO ℓ_1
                 statement-sequence$_1$
                 GOTO ℓ_2
         ℓ_1 statement-sequence$_2$
         ℓ_2 statement-sequence$_3$

      (d)   ON (numeric-expression) ℓ_1, ℓ_2, ℓ_3
         ℓ_1 statement-sequence$_1$
                 GOTO ℓ_4
         ℓ_2 statement-sequence$_2$
                 GOTO ℓ_4
         ℓ_3 statement-sequence$_3$
         ℓ_4 statement-sequence$_4$

        Any of the above statement sequences may be null, and the statement label moved accordingly.

[CNTRL-2]   STOP and RETURN statements may only be used as the last executable statement of a main program, function, or subroutine.

[CNTRL-3]   A FOR-loop variable may not be assigned a new value within the range of the FOR-loop, and may not be used after execution of the FOR-loop without reinitializing its value.

[CNTRL-4]   GOTO statements may not be used to transfer control to a nonexecutable statement.

Dimension Statements

[DIM-1]   All DIM statements in a module must be placed before the first executable statement.

[DIM-2]   All arrays must be explicitly dimensioned.

Functions

[FUN-1]   All single line functions in a module must be placed before the first executable statement.

[FUN-2]   A global variable may not be used in an expression referencing a function which uses that variable.

[FUN-3]   The formal parameters of a function may not be assigned new values within the body of a function.

Other Constructs

[OTHER-1]   Parentheses must be used to specify the order of evaluation for the components of compound logical expressions.

[OTHER-2]   All INPUT variables must be checked for errors upon data entry.

[OTHER-3]   Array structures may not be reformulated.

[OTHER-4]   All variables must be explicitly initialized before they are used on the right side of a LET statement.

APPENDIX B

Prettyprinting Standards

General Rules

[GEN-1]   The text of every comment line must begin with two asterisks and must not be aligned with surrounding program text.

[GEN-2]   All variables other than simple FOR-loop index variables must be specified in a comment statement.

[GEN-3]   Each external function or subroutine (level 2) called from the main program (level 1) must be listed immediately after the main program. Subsequent external functions or subroutines (level 3) called in level 2 must be listed just after level 2, etc. Within levels, the order is up to the programmer.

There are two allowed exceptions: (1) functions and subroutines called from several levels, and (2) functions and subroutines that are logically related (e.g., input-output routines). These may be grouped as desired by the programmer. For example, use the following:

```
        REM  **  MAIN PROGRAM, LEVEL 1
              . . .
             GOSUB 100
              . . .
             GOSUB 200
              . . .
             GOSUB 300
              . . .
        REM
        REM  **  LEVEL 2 PROCEDURES
        REM  **  SUBROUTINE 100
 100         . . .
             GOSUB 400
              . . .
             GOSUB 600
              . . .
```

```
          REM   **   SUBROUTINE 200
    200         . . .
              GOSUB 500

              . . .
          REM   **   SUBROUTINE 300
    300         . . .
          REM
          REM
          REM   **   LEVEL 3 PROCEDURES
          REM
          REM   **   SUBROUTINE 400

              . . .
    400       GOSUB 700

              . . .
          REM   **   SUBROUTINE 500
    500         . . .
          REM
          REM
          REM   **   SPECIAL PROCEDURES
          REM
          REM   **   SUBROUTINE 600
    600         . . .
          REM   **   SUBROUTINE 700
    700         . . .
```

Blank Lines

[BL-1]   Between each module (e.g., main program, function, subroutine, or block data subprogram), must be a page eject or a sequence of REM lines that is longer than the maximum sequence of REM lines within the previous module.

[BL-2]   The specification and the executable statements of a module must be separated by a sequence of REM lines that is greater than the maximum sequence of REM within the specification statements.

Indentation

[INDENT-1]   The executable statements in the body of each program and subprogram must be indented at least three spaces from the corresponding header and END statement. For example, modules may be indented as

> REM SUBROUTINE name (parameters)
> REM (title information)
>
> (specification statements)
>
> statement-1
> statement-2

.

.

statement-n

END

[INDENT-2]   The body of a FOR-loop must be indented at least three spaces from its corresponding header and terminating NEXT statement. For example, FOR-loops may be spaced as follows:

FOR I = 1 TO M

statement-1
statement-2

.

.

.

statement-n
NEXT I

[INDENT-3]   The body of an IF statement must be indented at least three spaces from its heading. For example, IF statements may be spaced as follows:

IF (logical-expression) GOTO ℓ_1
statement-1

.

.

.

statement-n
GOTO ℓ_2
ℓ_1 statement-1$'$

.

.

.

statement-n$'$
ℓ_2 statement-sequence$_2$

.

.

.

Local Spacing

[SPACES-1]   Relational and logical operators must be surrounded by at least one space.
[SPACES-2]   At least one space must surround each equal (=) sign.
[SPACES-3]   A space must be inserted after each element in a list of variables or parameters.

BIBLIOGRAPHY

[A1]   Armstrong, Russel M., *Modular Programming in COBOL*, John Wiley and Sons, New York, 1973.

[B1]   Baker, F. T., Chief Programmer Team Management of Production Programming, *IBM Systems Journal*, Vol. 11, No. 1, 1972.

[C1]   Cave, William C., *A Method for Management Control of Software Development*, CENTACS Software Report, No. 41, U.S. Army Electronics Division, Fort Monmouth, N.J., 1974.

[C2]   Chmura, Louis J., and Ledgard, Henry F., *COBOL with Style*, Hayden Publishing Company, Rochelle Park, N.J., 1976.

[C3]   Cougar, J. Daniel, Evolution of Business System Analysis Techniques, *Computing Surveys*, Vol. 5, No. 3, Sept. 1973.

[D1]   Dahl, O. J., Dijkstra, E. W., and Hoare, C. A. R., *Structured Programming*, Academic Press, New York, 1972.

[D2]   Dijkstra, Edsgar W., Goto Statement Considered Harmful, *Communications of the ACM*, Vol. 11, No. 3, March 1968.

[D3]   Dijkstra, Edsgar W., The Humble Programmer, 1972 Turing Award Lecture, *Communications of the ACM*, Vol. 15, No. 10, Oct. 1972.

[G1]   Goldstine, H. H., and von Neumann, J., Planning and Coding for an Electronic Computing Instrument—Part II, Volume 1, *John von Neumann—Collected Works*, Vol. 5, Pergamon Press, New York, 1963.

[J1]   Jensen, Kathleen, and Wirth, Nicklaus, *PASCAL User Manual and Report*, Springer-Verlag, New York, Heidelberg, and Berlin, 1975.

[K1]   Kernighan, Brian, and Plauger, William, *The Elements of Programming Style*, McGraw-Hill, New York, 1973.

[K2]   Kreitzberg, Charles B., and Schneiderman, Ben, *The Elements of FORTRAN Style: Techniques for Effective Programming*, Harcourt Brace Jovanovich, New York, 1972.

[L1]   Ledgard, Henry F., and Chmura, Louis, *FORTRAN with Style*, 1978.

[L2]   Ledgard, Henry F., *Programming Proverbs for FORTRAN Programmers*, Hayden Books, Rochelle Park, N.J., 1975.

[L3]   Ledgard, Henry F., and Cave, William, "COBOL Under Control," *Communications of the ACM*, Nov. 1976.

[L4]   Ledgard, Henry F., and Marcotty, Michael, "A Genealogy of Control Structures," *Communications of the ACM,* Nov. 1975.

[M1]   McCracken, Daniel D., *A Guide to FORTRAN IV Programming,* John Wiley and Sons, New York, 1972.

[M2]   Mills, Harlan B., *Mathematical Foundations for Structured Programs,* Technical Report, FSC 72-6012, IBM Federal Systems Division, Gaithersburg, Md., 1972.

[S1]   Spier, Michael J., *The Typset-10 Codex Programmaticus,* Technical Report, Digital Equipment Corporation, 1974.

[S2]   Strachey, Christopher, "Systems Analysis and Programming," in *Readings from Scientific American,* W.H. Freeman and Co., San Francisco, 1971.

[S3]   Strunk, William, Jr., and White, E. B., *The Elements of Style,* Macmillan, New York, 1959.

[V1]   Van Tassel, Donnie, *Program Style, Design, Efficiency, Debugging, and Testing,* Prentice-Hall, Englewood Cliffs, N.J., 1974.

[W1]   Weinberg, Gerald M., *The Psychology of Computer Programming,* Van Nostrand Reinhold, New York, 1971.

[W2]   Wirth, Niklaus, "Program Development by Stepwise Refinement," *Communications of the ACM,* Vol. 14, No. 4., April 1971.

[Y1]   Yourdon, E., *Techniques of Program Structure and Design,* Prentice-Hall, Englewood Cliffs, N.J., 1975.

[Z1]   ———, [ANS BASIC 1977] Proposed American National Standard for Minimal BASIC, American National Standards Institute, 1430 Broadway, NY, NY 10018.

INDEX

4971   05

BASIC WITH STYLE: Programming Proverbs
Paul Nagin and Henry F. Ledgard

"Programmers can and should write programs that work correctly the first time." This statement may sound idealistic to those accustomed to long hours of debugging. Yet it's the theme of Henry F. Ledgard's series of programming style guides. The latest addition to this popular series, BASIC WITH STYLE, is intended for BASIC programmers who want to write carefully constructed, readable programs. It offers short rules and guidelines for writing more accurate, error-free programs. These simple elements of style enable the programmer to focus creativity on the deeper issues in programming.

Among the topics discussed is the overconcern with microefficiency. A special chapter shows you how to use the top-down approach with BASIC. The guide introduces superior methods of program design and construction in BASIC. These proverbial gems will help BASIC programmers write programs that do indeed work correctly the first time!

Other Programming Style Guides by Henry F. Ledgard . . .

COBOL WITH STYLE: Programming Proverbs
Louis J. Chmura, Jr. and Henry F. Ledgard
Specifically for COBOL users.
#5781-4, paper, 144 pages

FORTRAN WITH STYLE: Programming Proverbs
Henry F. Ledgard and Louis J. Chmura, Jr.
Uses the new FORTRAN 77.
#5682-6, paper, 176 pages

PROGRAMMING PROVERBS FOR FORTRAN PROGRAMMERS
Henry F. Ledgard
Covers the original version of FORTRAN.
#5820-9, paper, 144 pages

PROGRAMMING PROVERBS
Henry F. Ledgard
Uses PL/1, ALGOL, and several other languages.
#5522-6, paper, 144 pages

HAYDEN BOOK COMPANY, INC.
Rochelle Park, New Jersey

ISBN 0-8104-5115